The New

Mary Lake & Port Sydney

1870 – 1940

by Ryan Kidd

Order this book online at www.trafford.com
or email orders@trafford.com

Most Trafford titles are also available at major online book retailers.

Printed in the United States of America.

ISBN: 978-1-4269-6470-1 (sc)

Trafford rev. 04/29/2011

North America & international
toll-free: 1 888 232 4444 (USA & Canada)
phone: 250 383 6864 ♦ fax: 812 355 4082

....to the 'Newcomers' who through their dreams, inspiration, and hard work made Port Sydney into the fine community that we cherish today ....

The Newcomers – Introduction

By the 1870's the trip from the old country to Canada was not nearly as harrowing as it was earlier in the century. Gone were the sailing vessels that took weeks and months to sail across the Atlantic. Gone too were the horrible living conditions causing death and disease that plagued the earlier emigrants. Steamships of course had made the difference. Trips could be scheduled and the ships were larger.

__THURSDAY SEPT. 9th 1869__ - We sailed at 2 p.m. Weather fine. We did not feel sick at all the first few hours. We were on deck all afternoon and enjoyed it very much. Towards 5 o'clock Mother went below. She said she did not feel so well as when she started. Soon after she came up again and asked me why I did not come to my tea. I went with her downstairs and looked at the tea and that was quite sufficient for me.
From 18 year old Annie Kay's Diary Appendix 3

The growth of the middle class in Britain also gave people the means to travel and settle more easily because they had more money to get started. Emigration to Canada was now something that many could attempt. The pictures that were portrayed of the new country were really flattering and many were enticed into making the passage.

The actual trip, however, was grueling. Poor living conditions resulting in sickness still existed. We are extremely lucky to have Annie Kay's diary of the journey and the first days here in 1869. Anne and her family were the first settlers in the Port Sydney area. They took up land about two miles south of Mary Lake along the Muskoka River.

__MONDAY OCT. 4th 1869__ - Father came home last Tuesday (Sept. 28th) from Stephenson. He has got 600 acres of fine land given to him. It is a few acres

5

short of the 600 but what he is short of in land is made up to him in water.
There is a lovely river running through our land and we shall have a bridge over
it next spring. There are thousands of cherry and nut trees on our land. They
gave me 100 acres because I was over 18 years of age.
From Annie Kay's diary – Appendix 3

Annie Kay's optimistic picture of the land and the forest belies the real conflict that faced all settlers coming to Muskoka. The word conflict has been used on purpose because life was tough for the settlers here. The basic theme of 'man against nature' was ongoing and filled their lives until they either found a way to conquer their environment or a way to make a living by providing services to others.

For some the harshness was too much and it defeated them. Discouraged, they moved elsewhere to where the life was easier. In the beginning many took advantage of the forests and made a living from the bounties of the land. A few found good soils beneath the forests and were able to farm after years of slugging work removing trees and boulders. Most found that the thin soils soon disappeared after the trees were removed and that their work was largely a waste of time. Those that remained soon discovered that they had to find other ways to make a living. The diary of Mary Butcher gives an intimate picture of life in port Sydney in the late 1800's.(Appendix 4) Ultimately the rough land and forests as well as the pristine lakes drew city people to that area and many new jobs appeared.

Part One

Part one of the book examines the lives of several families in Port Sydney who experienced this conflict and you will see how they met these challenges. It does so in the years after the first arrivals in 1868 and 1900.

The Clarkes

The Clarkes came from Balieborough, County Cavan in north central Ireland near the border of Ulster. Much of the county is covered with bog and forest. The soil is generally poor and the climate is damp and cold. Two thirds of those living there were tenants dependent on agriculture for their livelihood. They worked a patch of land rented from the landowner to make a subsistence living and they were almost totally dependent on the potato for food.

The agricultural economy of Ireland slumped after the War of 1812. Although there was a little recovery, further slumps occurred in the 1820's and early 1830's. During this time the population of the country grew and this made the problem of finding land for the younger sons even greater. The oldest son normally inherited the land. Stories of free land in Upper Canada were a great attraction to these land-poor young men. John Clarke (b 1810) had four older brothers who left Ireland for Canada during this time. By 1838 they were established and sent encouraging letters to John to join them.

Carngarve Ireland – Clarke House and attached barn

At this time most people lived in a tiny stone house. In the case of the Clarkes the barn was attached to the house both for convenience and protection for the animals. John would have left with some money in his pockets and since he already had brothers there, he stood a good chance for success in Canada. Three of his remaining brothers and cousins who stayed behind became doctors.

It is fortunate, however, that John left in 1838 before the potato famine broke out in the 1840's. Leaving was still a very sad occasion. You can imagine the heartbreak that must have been felt when he left for Canada as his family in County Cavan held the ritual "Living Wake". These were common rituals as families knew that they would probably never see their young sons and daughters again.

He joined about a million and a half others who left during this period. Britain encouraged emigration to Canada instead of the U.S. by reducing the fare to a cheap 15 shillings compared to the 4 or 5 pound fare to New York. The cargo sailing ships that were used in the five week trip were altered to accommodate the passengers. They packed bunks into vermin filled holds. Sometimes even empty fishing vessels returned to the Grand Banks with passengers on board. The trip was five weeks if they were lucky. Often, however, a ship could remain becalmed for weeks in the St.Lawrence alone. Passengers were expected to provide most of their own food and supplies but they rarely brought enough. Disease and death and burial at sea were common. Grosse Isle near Quebec City was the main reception centre in Canada. New arrivals were held there until it was sure that they did not have diseases before they were released to go further inland. It is estimated that 14,000 Irish are buried on this island. Most of the surviving men and women went to the cities. By 1851 more than half of the inhabitants of Toronto were Irish.

John Clarke must have been really relieved to get to Quebec City. Not only was he now in Lower Canada but also his brothers were not far away up the St.Lawrence in Hope Township near Port Hope Ontario. Although two brothers ended up moving on further west,

John, William, James and Robert Clarke were still likely living near Port Hope. One can imagine the welcome as they greeted their younger brother. Having his brothers there also meant that many of the hardships involved with getting started in the new land were eased. It was there too that he met and married Anne Gordon (b 1821) on November 15, 1838 and there that they soon began their family. The first two of their nine children were born in Hope Township, but by 1846 John's family struck out on their own and moved to a farm near Udora just south of Lake Simcoe. This was the common pattern among immigrants. These settlers, coming as they did from families who had never owned land, had a strong desire to get a piece of land for themselves. In Udora, John's family continued to grow until eventually there were six boys and three girls.

Through the 1850's and 1860' settlers continued to fill up the available land along the north shore of Lake Ontario until by the late 1860's new settlers began to go further west to the unsettled land of the prairies. This concerned the Family Compact Government of Upper Canada because the pine forests covering the lands inland meant royalties and income to them. The solution was to open these northern lands to new settlers who would in turn make the trees accessible to lumber companies as they opened up the farms. To encourage this, the government built settlement   roads.

SettlementRoads
p 185 Muskoka and Haliburton Documents 1615 - 1875

By the late 1860's these roads including the Bobcageon Road, the Muskoka Road and the Peterson Road that helped new settlers get into this part of Ontario. By 1858 a road had been built from Washago to Bracebridge.

Appendix One – Factually describes The Muskoka Rd. - Written by Commissioner P.M. Vankoughnet after whom the town east of Bracebridge is named. (excerpt below)

"Hence it will be seen that the Muskoka Road is, for 30 miles of its length, not only the highway to the section of land for the opening up of which it was directly undertaken, but also to that lying to the North-west, which is subsequently to be reached by the Parry Sound Road which branches off from it."

The government also actively recruited potential settlers in Britain to take up land in Central Ontario. There were Colonial Emigrant Aid Societies who produced brochures helping settlers by telling them when to come, when to build, how to clear the land and what crops to grow. There was even a Muskoka Settlers Guide. These settlers were about one third from other parts of eastern Canada, one third from Ireland and one third a mix of English, German and Scottish. Land agents like a Mr. Donaldson would meet them in Toronto and help them on their way north. The government also dropped charges for land to make it more attractive. Two hundred acres of free land went to the head of the family. Each family member over 18 got 100 acres and another 100 could be purchased at $.50 per acre. To avoid land speculation where the best land would be bought and sold later for a profit, settlers had to live on their land for six months a year.

For three of the four older sons of John Clarke the promise of cheap land was a great chance to begin their own lives further north. Thus it was in 1869 that Richard, Joseph and William Clarke struck out to make their fortunes in what is today Muskoka. The route that most took north included a steam boat to Orillia, then by foot to Gravenhurst, Bracebridge and on through the forests to the area that

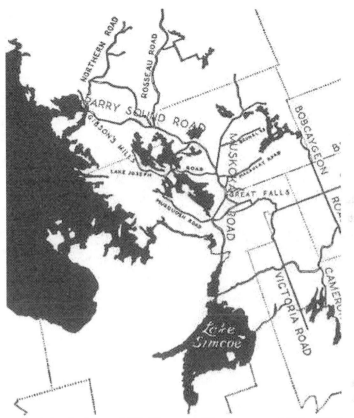

p 185 Muskoka and Haliburton Documents 1615 - 1875

was to become Port Sydney. The story goes that the three young men may have gone by canoe on the lower part of their trip and then they walked much of the northern part to Port Sydney. Not much is mentioned about the daylong walk from Bracebridge to Utterson along the stump littered road through the dense forest and swamp, or of the mosquitoes and blackflies.

See Appendix Two - **(A traveler's description of the Road in 1871)** "Oh! The horrors of that journey! The road was most dreadful...our first acquaintance with "corduroy" roads The forest gradually closed in on us, on fire on both sides, burnt trees crashing down in all directions."

(excerpt from Mrs King's Diary Appendix 2 p 24.)

A Log Corduroy Road Across a Swamp. They were incredibly rough, wagons frequently damaged wheels on them and horses broke legs.

What is remembered is their arrival at Mary Lake and of their spending the first night sleeping in blankets on the floor of Ladell's store. It was at this store where William first met Emma Ladell who would later become his wife. The three were to live part time with the Ladells for the next three years while they got established on their own land.

The three men took up farm lots 23, 24, and 25 in the eighth and ninth concessions. (See the map below)

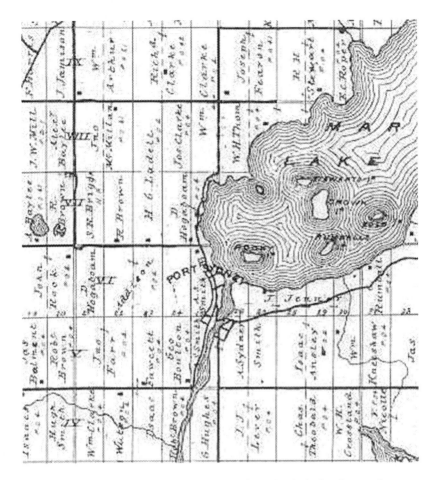

In the spring of their second year they had their shanty houses mostly finished. Unlike settlers in other areas there was a sawmill nearby. **John McAlpine** had built a small sawmill at the falls on the river south Mary Lake in 1868. John had come from Scotland and was the first settler in Port Sydney. He had built the first dam by driving in stakes along the side of a log that had fallen across the river just above the falls. He lived in a shanty at the east end of the present park at the falls. His life was rough and the story goes that he made bread by pouring water into the top of a bag of flour, kneading it until the water was all absorbed and then cooking it in a pan. Despite his rough life, John McAlpine cut much of the lumber for

13

many of the first homes in the area. He was also remembered because before the bridge was built he kindly helped people cross the river in his hollowed out log canoe. John did not stay long at the mill because of financial problems. He was bought out within a couple of years to absolve his debt.

John McAlpine's Mill c1869

The James Kay FamilyStory

One of the first families to reach the Port Sydney area was that of James Kay. They settled on land along the east side of the Muskoka River just below Stephenson Road Two. The school that was built at the corner of Stephenson Road 2 and Deer lake road was called the Kay School.

James Kay was born in the tiny village of Auchenhalrig in the northern Scottish highlands in 1814. Despite the fact that this was the time of Napoleon and the Duke of Wellington because of the distance from London, life in this remote village changed very little over the years. At the age of 25, James moved to Birmingham. The Duke of Richmond had procured a position for him as clerk in the

14

General Post Office. He held this post for thirty years. Five years after arriving at Birmingham, when he was 30, he married Anne Maria Room. She was the 25 year old daughter of George Room and Harriett Powell. James and his wife raised a family of eight children. Eventually, James was forced to give up his position with the post office on account of failing eyesight. The doctors advised him to give up working under gas lights and to get out in the fresh air and sunlight.

James had often thought he would like to see Canada. His older brother, Robert, was already living in Ontario and James had seen accounts of the District of Muskoka being thrown open for settlement and the free grant lands. James thus decided to move there. His two oldest sons, Jim and Will had already left for the "new world" so James, his wife, and four children prepared for the voyage. They left Birmingham and set out for Liverpool. The family then split up and traveled on two vessels. James, and his children Ellen, Agnes and Alfred sailed on September 4th, 1869 aboard the Steam Ship NOVA SCOTIAN and arrived in Quebec City on September 16th. Ann Maria and her daughter Annie Eliza sailed on September 9th 1869 aboard the S.S. MORAVIAN docking in Quebec City on September 19th. As can been seen in the picture below, these were steam ships with masts. They plied a regular route between Liverpool and Quebec City. Conditions on the ships were far better than those of the sailing ships of a few years before. Annie Kay, aged 18, wrote this diary to Mrs. Hands in Birmingham describing the trip.

Her diary is to be found at the back of the book as **Appendix Three.** It is a fascinating insight into the trip from England to Port Sydney

The picture below is from the Salem Collection in Massachusetts. It is the ship they travelled on although the spelling is different.

S.S MORIVIAN, 1864 Allan Line
courtesy: The Peabody Museum of Salem

The family settled on 600 acres in Concession 2 where they built their first house named after their previous home "Inverness".

Later they built a second home also called Inverness. The sketches were done by Alfred Kay

The first years were a struggle as they gradually cleared land to grow oats, potatoes, peas and turnips among the stumps. They sold their produce and milk to people in the town and to the nearby lumber camps. This income and the small pension that James had from the post office helped the family to get by. Alfred, who was one of the sons, became a well- known naturalist and taxidermist. His extensive collection of birds and animals is now in the Royal Ontario Museum. Annie Kay and her husband were the second couple to be married in the Presbyterian Church in 1885(now the United Church) and she helped raise $300 towards the first organ in the church.

So it was that the **Clarke** brothers returned to Udora in the spring of 1870 both to see their family and to get cattle to bring to their small patches of cleared land. The story goes that it was an incredible trip back north because the cattle did not want to be driven. An obstinate cow was a real handful particularly since if it wasn't watched every moment, it would take off into the forest and have to be tracked down. Forcing a cow across a swamp along a corduroy road would involve one son pulling on a halter and another behind twisting the cow's tail. I suppose that they may have drawn lots to see who would get to look at the backside of the cow. Those cows must have had tails that looked like corkscrews by the time that they finally arrived at their lands.

The next few years would have been ones of unremitting labour as the young men fulfilled the requirements to own their land. Each year they had to clear several acres, put up buildings the first year and do road work. Those who were short of funds often did the roadwork for others. If they fulfilled these requirements, they would ultimately gain title to the land. The quality of land on the Clarke brother's lots varied considerably. Because William's land (north of Belleview Rd.) was very rough, he soon turned to carpentry to add to his income. Richard and Joseph stayed on their farms until the 1880's. They then sold and moved northwest to Aspdin which was opening up at that time and where the soil was considered to be better. There, Joseph opened a store and Richard opened a sawmill. They were both instrumental in helping to erect the beautiful United Church in Aspdin. Their descendents still live in the area.

General Store owned by Joseph Clarke in Aspdin, early 1900's. Picture courtesy George Darling.

The Ladell Family Story

The background of the Ladell family was considerably different from that of the Clarkes. They came from Heachem in Norfolk, England where both Henry George Ladell (b 1823) and his wife Mary Ann (Spanton b 1824) had been respected merchants. Mary Ann had been a milliner (hat maker) while he was also a justice of the peace. They had first moved to near Pickering in 1858 and then in 1860 to Middlesex County near London, Ontario. It may be thought that they were adventurous to come to Port Sydney in their middle years in 1868 with a family of nine. Their family, however, was not healthy. Several in the family had consumption (TB) and they ultimately died early. Two of the men in the family died at the age of 45. They were the first of a number of families who came to this area to get away from the pollution of southern cities. People thought that the fresh clean air of the north would help them to recover from the deadly tuberculosis. At this time in England one in four deaths was caused by TB or its other name - Consumption. Even today it takes six to eight months to cure it with antibiotics. In the case of the Ladells the trip was too much, however, for their seventeen year old daughter,

19

Caroline who died along the way at Washago. One can imagine how devastating this must have been for the family. They brought her body with them and buried her near Utterson. Their neighbor **William Addison** also came for his health in 1878. He settled across the road from the Ladells. (See the map) He sold the land back to the Ladells in 1905 for $5.00. It was sold again in 1971 for $40,000. The clean air attracted many more people to the area as the years went on. It was also to be one of the reasons, along with the beautiful scenery, that encouraged the great period of Muskoka lodge building and tourism that began in the 1880's.

The Ladells were not farmers. They had men clear the land for their cabin and soon had a store operating on the north side of the road just east of the present Ladell Road. (lot 23 Con 7) It was here a year later that William Clarke and his brothers spent their first night in Port Sydney on the floor. The Ladells were Anglicans and held the first services in the new community at their house. They opened their store just in time because in 1869 a large group of settlers arrived in the area including the Clarkes, the Thoms, Jenners, Kays, Kneeshaws and Browns.

One of the big attractions of their store was the mail. Henry George Ladell would send one of his sons to the Post Office in Utterson to bring the mail back. To the lonely settlers, letters were a link to the outside world and to families back in Europe. They would eagerly gather at the store and exchange gossip and information as they waited for the mail to be sorted.

The Stage from Utterson and the Train

Despite these customers, it was evident that their store's location away from the lake and away from the important mill on the river would not be profitable. They were competing with the Hogaboam Store which was closer to the lake. **David Hogaboam** and his son had a store on the north side of the Utterson Road near the bend at the lake. Hogaboam was an enterprising person. He not only had lots 24 and 25 in Con.7 (on either side of Belleview St.)but also had a lot where Greer School is located and another 200 acres west of Utterson. He and his son were known to carry bags of seed potatoes from Washago on their shoulders. He also was the first Reeve of Stephenson Township.

David Hogaboam's Store (on the left/north side) at the lake

All went well until later in the 1870's when he suffered the fate of many who owned these early buildings. The owners would transfer heat from the fire throughout the upper part of the building by running stove pipes through these rooms. The soot collected in the pipes and was the cause of many fires. This was likely the reason for the fire that burned his store down. Soon after that he decided to sell his holdings and leave the area.

The Ladells were able to get a better location for their store from the new owner of lot 25 con 6 (the land across from the beach). Sydney Smith had come to the area in 1871 and bought the land where the village stands today as well as the land on both sides of the river. In 1874 he sold the lots west of Gore Street (across from the beach) to the Ladells for $10.50. It was a bargain for that price since the average value for a day's work in those days was $1.00. They built their new larger store on the westernmost lot.(at the corner of Hoth's Lane) It is said that the walls were made of 2 x 5 inch boards nailed side to side and that there were over 30,000 board feet of lumber in the building. Since their first store was located in a grove of Balsam trees, they called the boarding house part of the building the "Balsams." This new location became even more valuable because in 1874 the community had a "bee" to open a new road. A bush road following the route of the present road was cut and brushed from Indian Landing to the end of the Utterson Road where it ended at the lake in front of the store .This brought customers from the east as well as from the west. An interesting feature of the store and apartments was the water supply. They used the force of the water in the creek beside the store to power a pump which provided water in the building. This was very unusual in the days of hand pumps.

Ladell Store

There were major changes in the young village and in the lives of its inhabitants in these early years. Sydney Smith provided leadership in many ways including drawing up a plan for the streets and lots of the village. This plan was registered in 1873. Isaac Fawcett who helped him with this plan had a street was named after him. (see The Stores section)

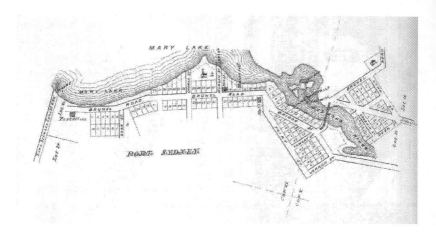

Since Sydney Smith was a staunch Anglican, he was also instrumental in getting the Anglican Church built. The minister at the time, Rev. Cooper collected money and prevailed on a Welshman named **Morgan** to build the church. William Morgan who had apprenticed in England came here via London, Ontario. A street in the village was named after him. Sydney Smith donated the land on the promontory overlooking the lake for the church. It was made of massive pine logs donated by many from around the lake. The construction began in the early summer and the building was sufficiently advanced to hold services in the fall. In the picture it is interesting to note that by 1873 there is not a tree in sight. The ladder on the roof was to get to the belfry as well as to get water to the roof in case there was a fire.

24

Christ Church c 1875

William Clarke, a staunch Presbyterian, and Emma Ladell, a good Anglican, were to be the first to be married in the church on October 21, 1873. In fact they had the marriage ceremony before the floor had been nailed down. Alan MacInnes and Rebecca Watson were to be the first married in the Presbyterian church in 1885.

William Clarke   **Emma Clarke (Ladell)**

The newlyweds lived at the Ladell store for some time before William was able to complete his house on a lot beside the store. His house is still standing across from the beach although it has been updated and modernized.

William and Emma's Home built in 1879

Over the next few years they had 12 children of whom 11 survived. Other than the three surviving boys, the daughters married into the major families in the area which means that the Clarkes became related to nearly everyone in the area. Two of the three boys stayed in Port Sydney. Arthur became a local contractor and built many of the cottages around the lake. As well, he managed the Village Inn for a number of years. The other son, Lewis, operated a sawmill north beyond the end of Belleview Road on the family land.

Lewis Clarke's Sawmill

Lewis died young and following his death, his wife managed the apartments in the Balsams. Later she built and managed Pine Lodge.

William built a barn behind the house where he could conduct his carpentry. Over the years he became known as a first class carpenter and cabinet maker. There he manufactured many of the doors, windows and frames for the houses springing up in the area. He freely volunteered his time to work on community projects like the Presbyterian Church (later called the United Church). The pulpit in the United Church is his work.

The Brown Family

In January 1869 Robert Brown and his wife Janet arrived in Port Sydney from Minto in Wellington County. Janet's family had come from Argyle in Scotland. She was first cousin to John McAlpine who had the mill on the river. He had told them about the free land and the good prospects in the area. They took up lot 22 of concession 7 next to the Ladells on the west. (See the map) Robert put up a house frame by June 1868. He then returned to Minto (Near Harriston Ontario) for his wife and their five boys and four girls. When they returned in the following January, they expected that the builder he hired to have put the roof on the house. They discovered that the house had no roof so they could not stay in it. As a result they had to live with the Haines family in Utterson for the winter. Over the years Robert bought other land in the area as can be seen on the map.

Many families suffered tragedies in those days. Their daughter Mary Brown died when she was young. Robert Brown decided to bury her within sight of their farm house in the new orchard west of the house. Over the years others from the community were buried there in the apple orchard as well. It was known as the Brown Cemetery until the family farm house burned in 1944. The Brown family then decided to donate the cemetery to the community. After that it has become known as the Stephenson Cemetery.

The Browns in the community today are descended from one of the sons named Hugh. In 1886 he married Sarah Annie Cheesborough Osborne. The origin of her unusual name is as follows. She was descended from Thomas Osborne who had been a missionary in the Bahamas before he moved back to Portsmouth, England. His son, her father, came first to Ohio and then to Con 2 Lot 13 in Stephenson Township. She was named after her step grandfather Rev. Cheeseborough who had also been a missionary in the Bahamas. Her father was the second township clerk and was a councillor for many years. He also ran the store in Utterson for years. Her sister was to marry Arthur Clarke mentioned above who was one of the two sons of William and Emma Clarke that remained in the village.

Hugh Brown became a successful timber cruiser for the Utterson and the Shier Timber Companies. It was his job to assess the types and value of timber on lots before the crews went in to cut down the trees. He did well by buying land with good stands of timber for himself over the years.

The Shier Lumber Camp

The Shier Lumber Company operated out of Bracebridge and had camps east of here in Brunel Townships. In the picture, the men are holding cant hooks which are used to roll logs. It is an indication of the importance of the cooks in the camp that they are in the centre of the picture.

Hugh moved into the distinctive stone house across from the beach in 1894. The first floor had been built in 1886 and the second floor with its distinctive mansard roof was added 1902 when Hugh bought it. The wall on the street was added about 1919. Hugh and Levi Stanworth built the wall all the while having loud discussions and arguments about politics, much to the amusement of the community.

Hugh and his wife lived in the house until 1925. Since then it has been used by their descendants during the summers.

Hugh Brown's House

The 1870's

There were many firsts in the growing community during this 1870's decade. The first community hall was built in 1876 on the west side of the road on the hill east of Morgan Road. They called it the Music Hall because of the many recitations and concerts that were held there. Often readings of Shakespeare, plays, concerts and dances were held at the hall. Mrs. Ladell and Sydney Smith led the grand parade for the opening of the hall.

Location of Hall

Events at the hall along with a fife and drum band, a cricket team and barn raisings created a lively community atmosphere. In each season there was at least one large concert or festival as well as numerous teas, bazaars and garden parties. These were particularly important in the long winters. A cricket team that played in a local league indicates the strong British influence in the community. The team played other local teams as far away as Bracebridge. The hall was the centre of life and culture for the village. The story goes that the hall was up on pillars at the corners and cold air flowed up through the floor boards. In the winter there was often a fog above the floor where this cold air met the heated air in the hall. It unfortunately was destroyed by fire about 1910. For a few years the second floor of the cheese factory on Morgan Street was used as a replacement until a new hall was built at its present location in 1925.

The lock between Mary Lake and Fairy Lake was begun in 1873 and completed the following year. The lock worked fine although there were ice damage problems over the next couple of years. The new lock made Port Sydney a key terminus for travel into the area.

Lock with Cottrill's Mill in the Background

Until the railway came further north in 1886, Port Sydney became an active port as travelers and settlers embarked to go to the northern lakes. The "Northern" side wheel steamship was launched on June 18, 1877 with great fanfare. Its length was 80 feet and it had a beam of 24 feet. It carried passengers to Lake Vernon and Fairy Lakes until it was finally replaced in the 1890's. The construction took place in the garden of Sydney Smith on the east side of the mill pond above the dam. The low flat land at the north side of the mill pond was used to beach steam boats like the Gem in the wintertime.

The Northern at the Dam. It was built on the shore behind.
Sydney Smith's house and barn are in the background

The customers coming to and from the sawmill and gristmill (seen in the foreground above) created unique economic opportunities for commerce. Store owners soon located here**. (See "The Stores" following)**

Tragedies in 1879 and in 1881 almost destroyed the young community. In both years serious fires tore through the area. The settlers cut down the trees, piled up the logs and brush and then burned the pile. The piles of logs would smolder for days. One hot afternoon in the summer of 1881 one such pile of brush west of the village was whipped into flames by a strong westerly wind. It wasn't long before sparks and embers were blown into the nearby dry trees and brush. Soon an inferno was created and the heat from the fire created its own wind. You can get an impression of the strength of the wind when you consider that embers were carried across the water to Stewart Island (Isle of Pines) Crown Island and Rocky

Island where fire burned the trees to the ground. Villagers abandoned their homes and stood in the lake with wet blankets over their heads. They held their children and babies up and tried to keep the blankets dampened amid the swirling smoke. You can imagine the fear and concern that they would have had as they watched this conflagration near the homes and barns that they had worked so hard to build. When darkness fell the fire died down as the cooler night air slowed its destructive path. In the morning they saw that the whole landscape changed. The countryside had become bare. William Clarke's barn was burned to the ground. For years afterwards the evidence of this disaster showed in denuded pictures of the lake and even today there are places where a black layer of carbon can be seen in the soil.

Treeless Rocky Island in the distance

The Stores

From the time of McAlpine's first mill, the economic engine of the town was at the falls on the river. The sawmill and the gristmill brought people from the surrounding country to the town. They had trouble reaching the mills because they were in a valley. In the east farmers and lumbermen had to negotiate a steep hill on Fallsview Road. The large sand and gravel pit along that road is a testament to the problems of guiding teams of horses over this section particularly

in the winter. Men called sandpipers built fires to heat the sand in the
winter so it could be thawed and spread on the road to slow down
the logging sleighs as they went down the hill. In the 1870's a bridge
was built across the river from the bottom of that road to the flats
on the west side and then up the hill where it joined the present road
at Fawcett Street making it an ideal location for stores.

The bridge can be seen at the right side of the picture. This bridge,
regularly undermined by the spring floods, was finally washed out in
the late 1880's. It was replaced by a wooden bridge near the present
site and finally by a steel one in 1898. Its piers can be seen just
downriver from the present one. The short-lived Goodwin store can
be seen farthest to the east. The stores at the top of the hill on the
west side, however, lasted for much longer.

Oxen on the Iron Bridge c 1900

The Fawcett Store

The first store on the west side of the river was Fawcett's. The family emigrated from England settling in what is now Scarborough. One son, Isaac and his wife, Emily after settling first in Holland Landing moved to Port Sydney in about 1869. Over the next ten years they had six children. Isaac soon began what was to become known as Fawcett's store. The store was located at the southwest corner of Fawcett Street and Muskoka Road Ten. The street had been named for him because Sydney Smith was grateful for his help in developing the street layout for the town. In a town meeting in 1874 David Hogaboam was the one who wanted the name of the community to include the word "Port". Isaac Fawcett was the one to move that the village be called Port Sydney and thus established its name.

From the description in a book called "The Night the Mice Danced the Quadrille" the store was a thriving enterprise. Getting supplies was an on-going problem because they had to be brought in by wagon from Bracebridge over roads that were not much more than tracks through the bush. The author of the above book, was a youth when he worked for the Fawcetts. He describes leaving for

Bracebridge at dawn and not getting back with a wagon full of supplies until midnight. The author also felt that he had earned a lot of respect from Mr. Fawcett to be trusted with so much money to buy the goods. Finally he describes leaving his job with the Fawcetts when Mrs. Fawcett decided that he was a good candidate to become the husband of one of her daughters. He was not ready to get married and so he left rather abruptly.

Fawcett Store seen in the 1980's before it was torn down

The building as seen here was considerably changed from the original by **David Jones** He raised it one storey to make it three stories and added the large kitchen at the back. He also added a lot of hardwood flooring and wainscoting. The original store had an entrance on the north side from Fawcett Street and it would have been on what is seen as the second floor.

The Jones lumber camp - Lucille (Jones) John Stevenson and David Jones

David Jones bought the three front lots and the three back lots as well as the building from the Fawcetts on January 12, 1888 for $550. Isaac and his family had decided to move back to Holland Landing on Lake Simcoe to be closer to their family. David Jones had been married to Elizabeth Nickason who died in 1895 at the age of 33 likely in childbirth leaving him to raise the children. Neighbours in the community took in several of the children including Lucille and raised them while he worked in his lumber camp part way to Newholm in the east. This was a common practice in those days when there were no social agencies to help. It was also a measure of how close knit these communities were and how everyone unselfishly helped one another. Jones's daughter Lucille later worked at the camp as a cook in the winters. (seen above) Her husband, John Stevenson came from Baysville. His parents, the Stevensons and the Forsythes were immigrants from the lowlands and highlands of Scotland.

Some of the men employed at the camp were Indians from the Menominee tribe. They produced beautiful moccasins in their spare time. These were prized gifts brought home by the men as

Christmas presents. Wrestling was a favourite sport. The Indians were really good at it and there were on-going tournaments when they had some free time. Despite the hard work and days that started as early as four am., the men were happy to make $25. per month. The money made it possible to buy supplies for the next year when they returned to their land and shanties that they were hoping to make into prosperous farms.

Lucille and John moved into the old Fawcett store in 1933. Their daughter lived there until 1986 when the town tore the building down because it was dangerously close to the road.

The Chester Store

The second of the three stores is the Chester Store. It is across Fawcett Street from the Fawcett Store and can be seen further up the hill from where it originally was located.

The Chester Store

Originally it was close to the street and at the north side of the lot next to the Butcher house with the narrow side of the building facing the road. Mr. Hay opened the store around 1888 and operated it until the Chesters took over in January 1892 when he moved to Meaford. The Chesters in turn ran it until December 1903 when they moved to Huntsville. Mrs. Chester was an accomplished pianist who taught many of the village children how to play. They, their two sons and a daughter were an active part of the village scene and were well-liked. The store was part feed store, part hardware and part grocery. They even sold pianos. These stores were information and gossip centres as they are today but the atmosphere was much different from today's stores. When you entered the store, the smells would strike you right away. The floors were oiled; butter and rounds of cheese would be out; coal oil would be sold; fresh leather harnesses would be displayed; bags of feed and grains would be open; hardware and tools were for sale. Men were there who had come from the barn and people were lucky to have a bath once a week …all these aromas and the smell of pipe tobacco and in the winter drying wool clothing plus wood smoke from a fire would confront the visitor immediately.

In 1934 the Wingfield family from Toronto bought the building and decided to turn it into apartments. Apparently they thought that it was too close to the road and the Butcher property so they decided to move it up the hill where it would also have better access to Fawcett Street. The whole community turned out over several days to watch the operation. The building was placed on skids and initially turned ninety degrees before it was dragged up the hill to its present location. A windless like the capstan on a ship used to bring in the anchor, with horses to power it, was used. The kitchen from the old building was made into a house which sat on the lower corner of Fawcett Street until recently. Miss Willis lived in it for many years before the Chesters moved back into it.

The Butcher Store

The last of the three stores at this location was the Butcher Store. The main building is still there. A grandson Phil Rumney and his wife Joyce live there today. The store was operated by George and

Mary Butcher from 1903 until the early 1920's. By that time the mills of Sydney Smith were only operating part of the time. As well the village had acquired a new centre where the present general store is located. It was run by the Watsons and later by their son Bill and his wife Clara Watson.

George Butcher came from the Isle of Jersey in the English Channel. He had four children by his first wife before she died circa 1887. Those children were to go to places as far away as Alberta, New Zealand, Australia and England. George worked at many different jobs and sold wagons, sleighs, reapers, and sewing machines to the community before he later decided to open a store in 1903. **(see diary below)**

The house that you can see here today was built by a man called Geall. He sold this house to George Butcher circa 1879. Mr.Geall had bought the deed for the land from Sydney Smith for $20. Mr.Geall also built the historic stone cottage on Deer street.

After his first wife's death, George soon married Mary Coldwell by whom he had five daughters. It is from the marriages of these daughters that familiar names in the village like Rumney and Dent originate. Mary who began a diary in 1892 kept it up until her death in the late 1920's. Although parts of the diary have disappeared, the remaining entries give an excellent picture of life in the village during the 1890's. **(see Appendix Four)**

The Butcher Store opened in 1903 when the Chesters moved to Huntsville and closed their store. It was in a building added to the north end of the present house. Alan MacInnes built the basement under the buildings. The basements helped to keep the buildings much warmer and provided a place to store goods.

The store seen to the right(north) of the house

The Butcher store closed in the early 1920's after which the centre of Port Sydney moved west to its present location. In the late 20's Mary spent two winters in Alberta with her step son Charles Butcher Charles who had married one of the Thoms girls mentioned in Mary's Diary had gone west to Bittern Lake in Alberta where he joined several others from Port Sydney. Descendants of the Ladell family and also the Roper family still live in that area. It was felt by many of these expatriates that the dry climate of Alberta was better for their health.

Members of the Butcher family have continually lived in the house in Port Sydney since those far off days.

Mary Butcher's (Coldwell) Diary (see Appendix Four)

The diary is over 600 pages in length and so several pages of sample entries over the period from 1891 to 1896 are included in the appendix to give the reader a feel for the diary. Since diaries are personal documents, a different person might well have written about other activities and interests. Below is a summary of the family's activities over that period as described in Mary's diary. The entries are mainly about her life, that of George Butcher their growing family, their friends, and what was happening in the community of Port Sydney. For your convenience, this information is summarized below and has been grouped into four areas: Work, Health, The Household and Socialization with the Community.

Mary Butcher and Evelyn c 1891

Work

George Butcher worked hard to keep the family solvent. Long before the store opened, he was an agent for many businesses that sold goods to local people. He travelled far around the surrounding countryside to sell these goods. There is frequent mention of him going to Huntsville, and places like Aspden and Ufford to sell mowers, reapers, sleighs, wagons, organs and later, sewing machines. Because travel was so important to him, there is mention of the annual problem of impassible roads in the spring. He like many around the community depended on money coming each year from family members in the old country. These funds were called remittances. To help tide the family over, George also regularly took on jobs like unloading rail cars in Utterson, buying bark for the tanneries, piling wood at the lumber yard and being a watchman at the mills.

Health

As a mother Mary was very conscious of health issues with her family. It is frequently mentioned that her children had colds and the grippe (Flu). Houses of that time were poorly insulated. They were often on pillars of rocks at the corners allowing cold air to blow under them. It is no wonder that the children were frequently ill. The occasional outbreak of typhoid and smallpox was much more serious. On many occasions the doctor would come out to their home even in the middle of the night. When diphtheria struck the town, the children were hastily taken to Mary's father's home in Allansville to get them out of harm's way. Toronto was distant, but when necessary, the children were taken there by train for really serious problems. Mary seemed to have easy births although a midwife coming in was mentioned. This was not the case with all of the women in the village. Several women died at or near childbirth leaving a young family behind. In those cases there is mention of others in the village taking in and raising the young children. It was a tight- knit village and they helped each other out in many ways.

The Household

With a growing family, a regular stream of guests and people occasionally staying over, Mary frequently speaks about food and getting supplies. The Chester store was next door and there was at least one weekly trip to the Ladell store for mail and supplies. She kept a garden for potatoes and fresh vegetables. Local farmers would also come by to sell produce. The Butchers often kept a cow and it would be let out to forage in the spring. This would mean that the family would later have to hunt for it to bring it back home. There were always problems about keeping food cool either by using ice from the ice house, root cellars or damp cloths. In the late summer they picked berries from Smith's and Jenner's Swamp in Bridgedale and east of it. The boisonberries were put down in preserves for the winter. Duck hunting and deer hunting were regular events in the fall. There were not as many deer around as today and hunting parties frequently came home empty handed during the short hunting season at the beginning of November. A pig was killed in the late fall to provide meat for the winter. Sewing to make clothes was an on-going task. When the Singer sewing machines appeared in the late 1890's the task became easier but it still took a lot of time. The weekly washing using rain water and getting clothes dry in damp weather or when it was really cold was a regular hassle. The spring and fall housecleaning was a serious concern for Mary. As soon as the ice went out, a week would be spent in cleaning each room from top to bottom. The same would also occur when a room had been used for someone who was sick.

Socialization With The Community

The Butchers had people in or visited with others two or three times a week. These people or friends of their children would come by often for tea or supper and would occasionally stay over. Mrs. Chester next door was a gifted pianist and they frequently mention going to hear her play. It is interesting how far they travelled. They were friends with the Dodds who lived quite far in on Candytown Road and with the Thoms who lived at the head of the bay north of Buckhorn Point. Mary's girls and the Thoms girls would walk around the southwest end of the lake, up Belleview and through the bush trail. There were a regular series of dinners, concerts and festivals throughout the year. These were particularly important in the long winters. Planning and preparations went on for days making the preparation, social occasions in their own right. In the same way Mary would mention going to church two or three times each Sunday. Both Mary and George belonged to several societies including the Women's Auxiliary, the Women's Institute, the Masons in Huntsville and even at one time a social organization called The Macabes. The whole town would turn out for political rallies and George was on the board of the Cheese Factory.

The Gem

When the steamship "Gem" was launched in 1897, it was much easier to visit around the lake and travel to Huntsville. This improved transportation allowed their social life to expand further. Over the years there were several ships called the Gem each replacing its predecessor.

Wedding Picture of Mary Coldwell and George Butcher 1888

Mary Butcher's Diary is a fitting way to end the first thirty years of Port Sydney. She provides real insight into the work and social life in this growing community. She shows the emotional and physical strength as well as the humanity that made this collection of pioneers into a community of caring and involved citizens. The newcomers of the 1870's were now veterans.

Part Two Introduction

The period between 1900 and 1920 was marked by two major changes in our community: tourism and the war. The arrival of tourists and construction of lodges on Mary Lake had been heralded by tourism promoters and the grand lodges on the big lakes of Muskoka in the 1890's. People in the large American cities south of the lakes as well as Toronto and Hamilton fled the summer heat and smog for the beauty and tranquility of the lakes. Many also came north to avoid the possibility of polio and tuberculosis in the cities. These well-to-do middle class people took the trains north to our area. One of the largest of the lodges not described in the previous book was Grunwald and its mysterious demise in 1918.

This period also marked a change in how the settlers viewed nature. For many the struggle to eke out a living was still a personal conflict in an attempt to overcome the barriers that nature presented them. Many from the cities, however, had come to appreciate the value of clean air and water. These people sought to live in harmony with nature and appreciate its beauty. The economy of the community began to cater to these city people and their view of nature.

Of course the most important event in these decades was World War One. It was to change the lives of the young men in our area in many ways including transforming them from their lives as the sons of the first settlers to world travelers and experienced men. On their return they were not content to maintain the ways of the sleepy village. They wanted change. These changes were to form the basis of the growth of Port Sydney into a separate village in the 1920's and 30's.

Grunwald

The story of Grunwald is the story of William Gall (1866 –1944). William was from Bradford England as was his wife. She was a descendant of the Rumball Family who were also from Bradford, England and were a well-known family around Port Sydney. Her father Charles was a leader in events at the Music Hall Community Centre and he had a farm just east of the town. What is now known as Forest Island was once known as Rumball's Island and the farm was on the mainland east of it.

William Gall seen with his family

William Gall first came to Waterloo and then later moved to Orillia where over the years he managed some of the largest hotels in the area and around the lower Muskoka Lakes. After briefly settling in Newholm, he bought a 100 acre farm on Rowanwood Bay. By 1901 he and his family had established their home on the west side of the lake. In the October 18th edition of the 1901 Huntsville Forester it was reported that William had decided to build a large summer resort on Rowanwood Bay that would accommodate about 100 guests. He was able to announce this because he had made arrangements to have a connecting ferry service with the Grand Trunk Railway in Huntsville where guests would arrive. They then would transship to the steamer "Joe" to bring them down through the locks to Rowanwood Bay.

The Joe seen at the Clyffe House Dock

William Gall was optimistic that his resort would be successful. He had many contacts from his past experience in the grand resorts of Muskoka. These summer resorts had attracted many who wanted to escape the grimy, smog- filled cities around Lakes Ontario and Erie. By starting to build late in the fall he was able to hire local people who could help in the construction after the crops were in and before winter jobs took them to the forest. During the winter, the local Women's Auxiliary made a large number of comforters and quilts for the new resort which was to be called Greenwald. The name was to remind customers that Muskoka was like the green hills of Switzerland. By the grand opening of the resort on July 4 of 1902 the name had been changed to Grunwald which means the same thing. Perhaps he was also hoping to attract Europeans who would see this experience as an adventure offered by the "new" world.

On July 4, 1902 the Huntsville Forester reported:

"The weather for Coronation Day was very inclement and interfered with the attendance at the opening of Grunwald Summer Resort on Mary Lake. A large crowd, however, was not to be set back by high winds and showery weather for each boat that left the Huntsville wharf carried a fair load of passengers and all reported a highly enjoyable day. The proprietors, Messrs Gall Bros. had made every arrangement for the comfort of the guests. The large resort was thrown open from cellar to garret, and the freedom of the place at the disposal of the visitors. The location is beautiful, situated as it is on a green sloping bank about two hundred feet from the shores of Mary Lake where the steamers land. Every care has been taken to make the building itself a model resort. Wide verandas have been placed on the side facing the lake from which a delightful view may be had. The superior dining room is one of the commendable features of the house. It is situated on the ground floor and is large enough to accommodate 100 persons. The bedrooms are large, cheerful and airy while the smoking rooms and parlours are ease and comfortable par excellence. A well stocked bar is also run in connection with Grunwald. It is now complete. A special daily boat service will at once be inaugurated by the Huntsville, Lake of Bays

50

and Lake Simcoe Navigation Company whereby passengers from the south, arriving on the Muskoka Express, may reach Grunwald the same evening at 6:55 o'clock. The prospects of the season are very bright."

On either side of the walkway from the dock and the beach to the front porch was a lawn used for croquet and tennis. Water pumped from the lake to the cistern on the hillside behind provided water for the lodge. An acetylene plant also brought bright lighting to all of the rooms.

Advertisements of the time claimed "a few weeks spent at Grunwald will restore the bloom to the pale cheek, will bring back lustre to the eye, impart spring to the step, courage to the heart and a deep gladness at being alive...."

Grunwald was a great success. So much so that a year later an addition had to be made. Sixty- four families had to be turned away that July. Sydney Smith from Port Sydney even loaned his houseboat to help accommodate the overflow guests. The charges were between $8 and $14 per week.

Sydney Smith's Houseboat Seen at The Mill

By 1907, however, William Gall had become overextended and was bankrupt. A combination of a short season, heavy maintenance costs and bank loans caused the failure. In 1908 he sold the resort to Mr. J.W White, an entrepreneur who owned a hardware in Huntsville. It must have been devastating for the Galls to give up their dream lodge. They ended up moving to Huntsville where they lived on Fairy Street.

Like many of the great resorts of Muskoka, Grunwald burned to the ground. On November 21, 1918 it was gone. Because its name was Grunwald and because it burned down so close to Armistice Day, there has been a rumour around the lake for many years that there was arson involved. This is clearly false as there never was any European involvement other than that the beautiful hills of Muskoka reminded many people who were new to our country of their homelands overseas. Descendants of the Gall family still own land around Rowanwood Bay and the great lodge is but a memory except for the crumbling resort cistern which still remains hidden on a nearby hillside.

The Grunwald Cistern

World War One

Oh! Oh! Oh! It's a lovely war,
Who wouldn't be a soldier eh?
Oh! It's a shame to take the pay.
As soon as 'reveille' has gone
We feel just as heavy as lead,
But we never get up till the sergeant brings
Our breakfast up to bed.

The optimism that is expressed in the song surged through Canada in 1914. Young men thought that the war would be over soon and some were disappointed that it might be over before they got there and were able to do their part. Many young men in Muskoka immediately joined regiments. Little did they know what was to come.

Lt.-Col. Donald McKenzie Grant (1868 - 1963)

As the war dragged on the need for more men increased. In Muskoka **Lt. Colonel Donald McKenzie Grant** organized the drive for enlistment. Grant was born in 1868, went to school in Simcoe and later Osgoode Hall. Before being called to the bar in 1891,he taught school in South River. He was married to Margeurite McLeod and practiced law in Huntsville for 70 years.

In later life he organized the Northern Ontario Volunteer Fireman's Association, was an elder at St. Andrews, a Past Master Mason, in the Horticultural Society, Orange Lodge and Literary Society, a lacrosse player and active in the Ontario Rifle Association.

As a Lieutenant in the 35th Simcoe Foresters and later its CO, he convinced the Federal Government to organize County Battalions. When the 122nd Forestry Battalion was organized with its headquarters in Huntsville in 1915, Lt. Colonel Grant became its Commanding Officer. He was directed to raise a regiment in Muskoka. By this time many young men in Muskoka had already joined other regiments. Despite this, by the summer of 1916 through the co-operation of the public and the efforts of Grant and his officers, the Muskoka Forestry Regiment was operational as part of the Canadian Expeditionary Force. It was ready to respond to the appeal from Britain in early 1916 for troops to undertake lumbering operations overseas.

The eligible men of the area had been sent literature about enlistment along with a card to send back explaining non-enlistment. The first reply for non-enlistment was given as follows: "Sorry to say I am overage, 53, also deaf."

While they were preparing and training the soldiers were billeted in local homes where the board provided was $4.20 per week. Privates received $1.00 per day while sergeants were paid $1.50 per day with fifteen dollars per month deducted from the pay of married men to go to wives. When privates were serving overseas, families at home received a separation allowance of $20 per month. Should the soldier die overseas, the widow would receive $22. per month with $5. per month for each child. By June 16, 1916 the Muskoka 122nd was 725 men strong.

WW 1 Veterans from Port Sydney Area

The names are followed by local information about them and their regiment. As you can see, many belonged to the 122nd but also many had already joined other regiments.

Albert Christopher Andrews —was a home boy with the Jenners at Clyffe House- the 122nd
Hilton Brown – Likely the son of Hugh Brown, lived in the stone house opposite the beach –Canadian Engineers
Wilfred Essen –The family had farms down the river south of port Sydney. He lived at the SE corner of Morgan Street and Muskoka Rd. 10 – the 122nd

The Gardiners George Charles and John lived at the end of Beaver Meadow Road. George Gardiner was sent to Russia at the end of WW1 as part of the International Brigade to defend the White Russians against the Red Russians 1918- 1920. 1st Central Ontario Regiment

The Henrys –Charles and John. Lived in Candy Town. One Married into the Trollip Family- 1st Central Ontario Regiment

Fred Hodges -104 Central Ontario Regiment

William Hopkins -194 Battalion

The Hughes- David, Malcolm, J.J.Stanley - Some of family still live south of Port Sydney-2nd Central Ontario Regiment

Geo Jaggard -Lived across from the old Butcher store- Transport

James Kay- lived south of Port Sydney along the river..one of the original families-the 122nd

Angus Keppy-The 122nd

Harold Ladell- born in Texas son of Arthur Ladell. Another son Wally was killed at Vimy-151 Battalion

Loys-Albert, Robert - Albert built the stone cottage on Ontario Street. –Navy and RCHA

McInnes Allan- builder in the village. Built and lived in house at the NW corner of Morgan Street and Muskoka Rd. 10. – 2nd Central Ontario Regiment

Nickasons Arthur and Ernest- Lived north of Deer Lake on Deer Lake Rd. One of the early settlers in Port Sydney 1869 – 1st Central Ontario Regiment

Walter Osman- one of his family married a Clarke The 122nd

Albert Phippen – lived east on Beaver Meadow road in Brunel – The 122nd

Edward Pinnington – a padre in the war, became a canon in the Anglican Church. Lived many years in Port Sydney. His two sons are buried in the Anglican Cemetery.162 Battalion

John Smith – linked to the Jones family and the Stevenson Family in Port Sydney. Lived in the old Fawcett store until the mid 1930's. Built a house between Fawcett Street and The United Church-The 122nd

John Thoms – brother of Dick Thoms was a sniper..grandfather of David Thoms – 1st Battalion

Harry Trollip – bought farm from the Rumballs Con 6 Father of Kay Cosman –The 122nd

Edgar Whitmore…lived in the NE corner of Ontario Street and Muskoka Rd. 10.He was a carpenter.

Canadian Nurses had served near the front in the Northwest Rebellion and the Boer War before WW1. In WW1 a quarter (2333) of Canada's Registered Nurses enlisted. After six weeks of training they were formally enlisted into the Canadian Army Nurses Corp with a rank of lieutenant. The majority served in hospitals in France, in England or on hospital ships. Aside from other duties they gave anesthetics in the hospitals and casualty stations. The following nurses came from the Huntsville area: Olga Bushfield, Margaret Duncan, Norma Fisher, J.Kehoe, Zoe Loy, C.Milton, Jean Moir, Maude Pym and Rena White.

June 1, 1916

On this day the three companies of the Muskoka Battalion broke camp in Huntsville and started on a 'trek' through Muskoka. The 'trek' was to show the battalion to the communities and to encourage others to join. They made quite a show as they marched west out of Huntsville with the Battalion Flags flying and the band playing.

The Colours are housed at the Bracebridge Courthouse

The papers of the time tell of hundreds lining the route and how many of the houses were decorated with flags. Telegraph poles along the way were placarded with "Join The 122[n.] At Madill Church local women provided milk for the 800 men.

At Port Sydney they pitched camp on Ladell's farm just east of the old fire hall. Again the whole community met them and cheered them on. They camped in their 'pup' tents. The battalion was on the move by 5:00am the next morning and on the road by 8:30.

The 122nd camp taken at Milford Bay June 14, 1916 (from the Schafer Album)

Despite the fact that there was a lot of rain during the trek, the crowds continued to line the roads to show their support. Whenever they camped as they travelled south to Bracebridge, Gravenhurst, then to Bala, Port Carling and Milford Bay, the communities brought them pies and even ice cream. Rather than marching from Gravenhurst to Bala, they went by steam boat. In the camps work continued as the men drilled. Wagon transports brought in supplies and repairs were made to equipment.

Despite this, life at Camp Borden must have been something of a shock after the carefree atmosphere of the 'trek' around Muskoka. There reveille was at 5:30 am, sick parade was at 6:00 am, breakfast was at 7:00 am, drill was from 8 am – 12 am with a 15 minute break, dinner 12:30, drill again from 2:00- 4:30, tea 5:30, retreat 7:30 and the last post at 10:00pm with lights out at 10:15 pm. Rumours abounded about where they were to be sent and when they would go. The 122nd wintered in Galt Ontario and shipped out to Nova Scotia in the spring of 1917 where they embarked on the SS Olympic and finally docked at Southampton England on June 10, 1917.

59

These young men from Muskoka were ideally suited to the forestry needs of the war. As the sons of the first settlers, they knew intimately how to produce lumber which was a vital necessity in the war effort. Those of the battalion who remained in England took down much of the forest of Windsor Park around Windsor Castle. It was one of the few remaining large forests in England. Many, however, went to France where they frequently worked under fire as they cleared land for airfields, laid down ties for railroads, built hospitals and barracks and constructed trenches. These Muskokan soldiers including those from Port Sydney experienced the full impact of that awful war far from the beauty of Muskoka.

Futility

(1918)

He pressed against the rough parapet,
Ankle deep in putrid mud,
Oblivious to the stench of filth and rot
Meandering through the trenches,
Home to:
Red-eyed rats --- fat and satisfied,
Blank-eyed soldiers --- gaunt and terrified.

Heedless of the horror below, a soft spring breeze
Unwittingly wafted Death's miasma
Beyond crater-pocked hell
Into the battle-ravaged town

.

Palms sweat-slicked, licking dry lips,
He waited---
The officer's whistle shrieked once,
Over the top, he sprang, bellowing,
Head low, rifle clutched, sprinting
Towards barbed wire tangles.

Machine guns clattered.
In mid-step, he paused, confused,
Features softening, rifle dropping,
He slid slowly into the slime.

In a gun's flash,
All dreams, all hopes extinguished.
Forever, nineteen,
His friends called him Jimmy.

Eleanor Kidd

Part 3. 1920- 1940

The years after World War One marked the beginning of a new era for Port Sydney. Increasingly the community saw its surroundings and the beauty of the lake as a new kind of resource. The people from the city came to this pristine setting in increasing numbers. They admired the beauty and purity of the setting. As the trees regrew and the landscape gradually returned to its original state, people came to the lake to build their cottages in their little pieces of paradise. They also wanted their children to have a chance to be a part of this ideal setting and so summer camps appeared.

The soldiers who had gone away as the sons of settlers from a small town returned as different people. Aside from the horrendous experience of the fighting, they also had learned new technologies and had become much more cosmopolitan by meeting others from all over the world. They were not content to return to try to make a living from the unproductive soils of Muskoka. By this time the jobs in the lumber mills had also dried up. The easily accessible primeval trees had been largely cut. Here and there were still patches of forest but since there was not enough business for the mills, they were closing. Around Mary Lake four mills had closed. In the Port Sydney area the only large patch of trees was in the Sydney Smith Forest in what is today Bridgedale. He had kept these trees as a personal reminder of the original forest. These were finally logged out in the early 1930's.

Logging Bridgedale

Cars became readily available to everyone during this period. Travelling to Muskoka was not just limited to those who came by train and stayed in the grand lodges as they did before the war. It was also a period of road construction such as Highway 11 which was completed in 1929. The lodges, which had been built before the war, flourished again. Around Port Sydney these were Clyffe House and Belleview Lodge (Belleview St.). Also from before the war were lodgings like The Balsams (at Ladell's Store), Fairview (next to the general store), Mary Lake Inn (across from the beach) and The McInnis house (Morgan St.). After the war and into the 30's almost anyone who had a big house took in lodgers during the summer. These included: Ferndale(Belleview St.), Pine Lodge, Mulvaneys (Greer Rd.), Marshalls (Greer Rd.), Spruce Lodge (Near Hiawatha Rd.) , Rosewood (The old Chester Store), Avon Lea (Across from the Beach), Broadview(Belleview Rd.), Victoria Villa (West of Pine Lodge) and up the lake, Rowanwood Lodge (where Grunwald was) , Arcadia House (across from MBC), Breezy Point (at MBC) and Muskoka Lodge (east of Snowshoe Island).

The Clarke Taxi at Ladell's Store

With the return to stability after the war, the lack of a community hall was a real problem. The second storey of the old cheese factory on Morgan Street was not satisfactory and had only been a temporary solution after the Music Hall had burned down before the war. The smell of the cheese was rank particularly on warm days.

The Cheese Factory

A committee of local leaders was formed from the people of Port Sydney to get a new hall built. They were referred to as the Ratepayers of SS# 9 the local school district. The school is located east of the bridge and is part of Rosewood Apartments. There were several meetings and the two sets of minutes enclosed in **Appendix Five** show who was involved and the key decisions. The land was purchased from Sydney Smith for $800 and the hall built for $3600. When the new hall opened on July 1, 1925, Sydney Smith and Mrs. Jenner led the grand parade through the town. He had led the parade fifty years before with Mrs. Ladell when the first hall was opened.

Sydney Smith was not well and was not to live long after the grand parade. On September 28, 1925 he had a bad cold which eventually became pneumonia and he died on Oct 2. The community was in shock. Since his arrival in Port Sydney nearly fifty five years before, he had been a prime mover in the affairs of the town. His mills had been the economic engine of the town for well over 30 years and he had personally supported many of the key people and institutions of the town. After a packed funeral at the Anglican Church, he was buried in Stratford, his original home.

He left a big gap in the leadership of the town but others were there to take on his mantel. As can be seen by the caliber of the men that helped to get the town hall built, there were people who were ready and willing to step up when needed and get things done.

The diseases that plagued the community in the late 1800's were still with the people of the village. In the mid 1920's one the Clarke boys caught small pox in Toronto. On the hill west of the bridge is a hole in the ground about 12 feet by 14 feet. Ernie Johnson and his family lived in a house there.

He was a wood cutter employed by Sydney Smith. In 1924 they caught diphtheria and they all died. The story goes that the house was burned to make sure that the disease did not spread. The hole in the ground is mute testimony to show that deadly diseases still had an impact well into the twentieth century.

Port Sydney was a force to be reckoned with on the sports field as well. In the mid 1920's the baseball teams particularly brought recognition to the community. They played teams as far away as MacTier and in 1926 they won the Muskoka Championship in a league that included: Huntsville, Sundridge, Parry Sound and Gravenhurst. Mel Clarke the son of Arthur Clarke, was the team leader and pitcher. They played on the grounds of the community hall and they must have had to run to the lake to retrieve 'homers'. Mrs. Brown who lived next door was so upset with players climbing her fence and retrieving balls from her vegetable garden that she used to confiscate the balls and thus end the games. Sometimes the cottagers also helped to pitch. Bill Rumney, Andy Beemer, Al Field and Wally Hall all took their turn on the mound.

The hockey teams from the town were also famous in the area. They played on a rink at the community hall. Their first year in 1926 the team carried water from the lake to make the rink. The next year Bob Jenner took pity on them and provided a gasoline pump to get the water up from the lake through an iron pipe that must still be in the ground. The team played in the Muskoka Rural League that included: Falkenburg, Windermere, Allansville and Milford Bay. Ivan Kirkness was a local teacher that helped the team pictured below. The influence of the Clarke family can be seen on the team.

Back Row L - R
Bill Clarke, Ivan Kirkness, Melville Clarke, Norman Vanclief, Hugh
Green, Edgar Johnston, Murray Clarke, Allan Clarke, Jack Smith
Front Row L - R
Walter Dent, Terence Clarke, Bill Kimmel, Bob Smith, Victor Clarke
1934 - 35   MUSKOKA RURAL LEAGUE CHAMPIONS

The Cottagers

In the years before the war, cottagers had begun to settle around the
lake. In some cases people who had visited the lodges liked the area
so much that they decided to buy their own piece of heaven. In other
cases they were attracted by a sense of adventure or the stories that
friends had told.

Birkswyld Cottage

Shortly after the railroad was completed through to Huntsville in the
1880s a group of teachers came north from Stratford to spend their
summer in Muskoka. Presumably they had heard stories of the Port
Sydney area from Sydney Smith's sister who lived in Stratford or
from Sydney Smith himself who usually spent part of the winter
there. Among the teachers were Frances and Emily Garden. They
took the train to Huntsville and then took a steamer down the river

to Mary Lake and thence to Mainhood's Warf. (later the site of Muskoka Lodge just east of Snowshoe Island)

They had rented the Rumball homestead just east of what is now known as Forrest Island for the summer. The house was called Springmount. Here the group can be seen at the house.

By 1890, they had formed such an attachment to the area that they bought land nearby on the lake. They had Arthur Clarke build the present cottage on the lot in 1904 making it arguably the oldest cottage on the lake. Since the cottage was originally surrounded by birch trees, it was called Birkswyld. The cottage was in the midst of Harry Trollope's farm. His house and hen house were to the north; his barn and vegetable garden were to the east (the barn is still there beside Muskoka Rd. 10) and his potato patch was to the south. His boat livery business and boat house were also to the south and became known as Hilarity Hall. It was named after a giant amusement park in Portland Oregon that opened a Hilarity Hall in 1918.

George, Emily and Francis Garden

Birkswyld originally had a boathouse, but after nearly 80 years it had to be removed. The cedar siding shingles, however, are still the original ones. Prior to WW 1 much of the provisions for Emily, Frances and their brother Jack came by boat from Huntsville or from local farmers. It was stored in a cold cellar dug into the hillside. In the 1920's, like other cottagers, an ice box was the way food was cooled. At the cottage the ice box was made of oak and lined with galvanized tin. Ice which had been buried in sawdust during the winter would be brought from the ice house next door at the Trollops.

Murray, Arthur and Vic Clarke cutting ice at the town dock

In 1933 electricity came to the area and to the east side of the lake in 1945. Along with it came refrigerators. Water from the lake was initially carried and later pumped up to a holding tank. Each bedroom would be equipped with a basin and a pitcher of water as well as the chamber pot under the bed. Laundry was done by a scrub board and a hand wringer. The impressions written by Norah Malone Garden…who married Jack's son Gordon **(See Appendix Six)** gives a more complete description of the interior of the cottage.

Jane Garden who presently lives in the cottage in the summer is the third generation of the Garden family to treasure it. Few of these original Muskoka cottages remain. They are a nostalgic reminder of the erstwhile days of 'cottaging'.

Down Memory Lane Cottages

Clyffe House had only been operating for a few years before the guests began to want to have a place on the lake of their own. Bob Jenner, the owner of Clyffe House, decided to take advantage of this and in 1910 had the area between the point and the cliff surveyed into nine lots. The first two cottages built on these lots were at the extreme ends of it. They were built within four years. The cottages along this stretch are described in "These Memories I leave to You". The style of cottages built before WW 1 often combined the cottage and a boat house like these two.

The Bell Cottage   **The McLauglin Cottage**

The two Bell sisters were teachers and stayed here for many years with their brother's son. The cottage was not torn down until the 1950's. They would come to Utterson by train and then to the cottage by horse and buggy driven by Arthur Clarke who operated a livery service. Like many of the cottagers along this stretch of shoreline, they ate their meals at Clyffe House.

Dr. John McLaughlin was a dentist from Cleveland. His daughter Jean played violin at the dances at Clyffe House. The cottage burned down in 1923. The Copp family, who were related to the publishing family in Toronto, replaced the cottage with the present one. They had been guests at Clyffe House and were one of the early members of the Yacht Club on the lake.

The cottages that were built before WW 2 from west to east along this stretch of shore were The McLaughlin Cottage, The Doran Cottage, The Field Cottage, The Ansell Cottage, (later the Wood Cottage) and the Bell Cottage

The third cottage to be built in this group was that of the Doran Family about 1912. It was the third from the west end. Although the Dorans lived in High Park Toronto, they employed a builder from New England. It featured large porches, five bedrooms and tongue and groove paneling in the interior. Once again there was a strong link between the family and Clyffe House. Unlike many of the cottages of the day it had a water system involving a hand pump and a tank which supplied gravity fed water on demand.

The Doran Cottage

The Ansell family owned the fifth cottage from the west and of the group and bought it in the 1920's. It was of a more traditional Muskoka design, but the Doran builder added dormers. Once again the Ansells had strong connections to Clyffe House and the son Ross Ansell even played on the Clyffe House baseball team called the "Invincibles."

The Ansell Cottage

The fourth cottage from the west end and the sixth one were built in the 1940's. The Field family owned a Knitting Mill near London and had visited several cottage areas around Ontario before settling on Mary Lake. They built a cottage using the 'Haliday' precut construction which was just becoming popular in the late 1930's. Mel and Vic Clarke put it together and Jim Smith who lived just east of the bridge, built the fireplace. Of all the cottages in this group built before WW2, this is the only one that remains.

The Field Cottage

The sixth cottage in this group (next to the Bells) again was built in the early 40's. It was owned by Charlie Wood who had been a WW 1 pilot and POW before he became a bank manager. It was later sold to the Reive Family.

The Wood Cottage

The Moodies

Between the river mouth and Clyffe House there are three large cottages. They were built after 1813 by Arthur Clarke for the Moodie and Stockford Familys. The Stockfords came from New York and were well-off. Their money came from their involvement with Standard Oil. Standard Oil was a giant company out of Ohio that operated from 1870 by the Rockefellers until it was broken up by antitrust laws in 1911.

When their daughter Grace married Charles William Moodie, the three cottages were started. The large centre one was used by the Stockfords. The smaller cottage nearer the river was built for the newly-weds. Charles was always known as "CW" and he came from an important family as well.

Grace and Billie

CW's father, John Moodie operated a knitting mill in Hamilton. He sent his son John Jr. to England to buy knitting machines that allowed the family business to expand. As well along with five other investors John Sr. brought hydro power to Hamilton in 1898. They

74

formed *The Cataract Power Co. Ltd.* and on August 25, 1898, hydro power was sent twenty seven miles from *DeCew Falls*, at St Catherines using water from the old Welland Canal. New industries such as the forerunners of the Steel Co. of Canada (Stelco) and Canadian Westinghouse were attracted by the cheap power making Hamilton the industrial centre it is today.

John Moodie Sr's family included three sons and a daughter. Charles (CW), Robert, John and Jean.

CW's brother John Jr. also played an important role in Hamilton. John Moodie invested in many businesses. He co-founded the *Eagle Knitting Co.* in Hamilton in 1888 with his father and brother James Robert. He was also president of the following companies; *The Royal Distillery* (Hamilton) for nine years, *Robinson Industries* (Hamilton), *Dover Industries* (Chatham, Ontario) and also, president of a company operating the Hamilton-Toronto steamer run. He owned the first player piano in Hamilton, owned the first bicycle in Canada (1878), owned the first motorboat in the Hamilton Bay and also owned the first automobile in Canada (in Hamilton 1898), a one-cylinder Winton he imported from Cleveland Ohio.

The third cottage, called the Oaks, to the east was built for their sister Jean Moodie around 1913 as well.

The Oaks

Jean never married but always had lots of friends, nephews and nieces at the cottage. To help look after things she had a companion, a cook, a handyman and Mel Clarke who frequently acted as chauffeur. Jean had busy summers entertaining and hosting picnics, children's parties and berry picking expeditions. Berry picking and preserving was still an important community activity.

Jean Moodie

CW was a great fisherman and really enjoyed Mary Lake and trips into Algonquin Park to fish.

CW at the wheel of his boat

CW left the westernmost and the centre cottages to his daughter Grace Jr. and her husband Grant Davis.

Jean willed the Oaks cottage to John Jr's grand daughter Mary (daughter of May Elizabeth and Victor Vallance). Mary had married Hugh Hand, another person from Hamilton. Hugh was the grandson of Professor William Hand who brought the first Canadian fireworks company to Canada from Hereford England. The company became famous for its huge tableau fireworks displays that were shown at the CNE. For nearly 40 years after the 1950's he is remembered for providing free fireworks for the Port Sydney Turkey Dinner display.

The Johnson Cottage

Despite a busy life in the community and at the mills, Sydney Smith kept up strong connections with his family and with his sister in Stratford. Each winter he would return there. It is not surprising therefore that he welcomed friends and family in the summers.

Thus it was that in 1916, that he invited his nephew (son of his sister Lucy) to Port Sydney. The Rev. Herbert Johnson and his wife Bessie and their six year old son George came that summer and were put up in the cheese factory which Sydney Smith owned.

Lucy Smith had married Herbert Munnings Johson who had come from Norfolk England in 1862. H.M. Johnson had been a successful cheese producer in Haysville (Near Stratford) and later insurance agent and financier in Stratford. His impact on Stratford is still seen through his role as a founder of the Stratford Parks Board and the beautiful parks in the city.

The visit by Herbert Jr's family in 1916 was successful except for one matter. When the cheese factory was hot on the summer days, it brought out the rank smell of cheese curd from the wood. The family stayed there for six summers and young George developed a strong life- long aversion for cheese.

Reverend and Mrs Herbert Johnson with Sister May at the Johnson cottage in the late 1930's. The Sisters of St. John the Divine summered at their retreat, Ballycroy, and were a regular sight on their evening strolls through the village. (G.H. Johnson photo)

In 1922 Sydney Smith gave Rev. Johnson four lots along the west side of the river above the dam. They had a cottage built on one of them in 1923 by Herbert and a parishioner. It was an open concept prefab clapboard building with a beautiful porch across the front that provided a great view of the lake and Rocky Island.

-**The Johnson cottage in 1935**, with boathouse construction underway to the right of the photograph. Much of the original cottage remains today, although the broad screened porch has been replaced by picture windows and a vaulted roof.(Johnson family album)

In 1935 Victor and Arthur Clarke built the brown boathouse on the river. It supplemented the dock along the rocks below the cottage and housed the family motor launch called "The Old Girl". They frequently went on evening excursions in the launch and occasionally on the Gem to the upper lakes including trips across south portage to Lake of Bays and by steamer to Bigwin Inn for lunch.

George Johnson and his mother in the 'Old Girl", a Minett mahogany launch built in Bracebridge in 1917 and acquired by Reverend Herbert Johnson in 1935. (Photo by H.J. Johnson circa 1936)

He almost never saw another boat out at night. George recalled in the 1920's how few lights there were around the lake. He said there would be a faint glow from the Thoms' farm in Thoms Bay, and another glow up the lake at the Lawrence farm (now Gryffin Lodge), but that was about it...nothing else but the light of the stars and the moon. There were very few cottages, and of those, few had electricity until the 1940's.

George Johnson found time from his job with the Financial Post to develop his knowledge and love of Mary Lake. This was expressed through his study of the Pleistocene Ice Age on the geography of the lake and his research and publishing of the important book on the history of the Mary Lake pioneers called "Port Sydney Past" produced in 1960.

The Thoms Bay Cottages
Dick Thoms sat on his porch overlooking Mary Lake and the bay that was known as Thoms Bay. From his vantage point he could see

the three cottages along the north side of the bay. They had been built by three teachers since the war ended in 1918. The closest one was the Flock Cottage; beside it was a big field where Dick occasionally grazed cattle; then came the Rogers Cottage and next to it was the Hogg Cottage. The cottagers would come by train to Utterson and then travel by car to the farm and finally row across the bay. There was a rough trail over the hill but it was hardly used. Even though the woman cottagers were younger, they were still good company for Dick's sisters.

Dick Thoms house c 1920

The Flock Cottage

Arthur Flock who taught physics at Riverdale Collegiate in Toronto first visited the lake in 1915 and was so enthralled with it that he bought 300' of shoreline from William Thoms. He told his colleagues and students about the lake's beauty so often that they came up to see the place. One of his fellow teachers bought a lot and one of his students also bought property there. Not only did Flock teach physics but he was also an artist who painted many lake scenes. As well he was also a keen naturalist and golfer. He regularly had guests and boarders. One summer a family rented rooms at his cottage while a daughter worked as a maid for Arthur and his sisters. That summer one of the family members killed a loon. Arthur Flock

81

was so upset that he gave the family three hours to get off the property.

He had built a two storey cottage in 1918 and 1919 similar to the McLaughlin and Bell cottages across the lake shown above. The building was over the lake with a boathouse underneath. It was built on silt and sand in the shallow water. This was an unfortunate location because during the ice break up in the spring it frequently shifted. Eventually the cottage was pulled out of the lake back up onto the shore using a winch like the one used at the Chester Store.

The Flock Cottage

The cottage had a pleasant upstairs sleeping porch, but the chimney which was added in 1926 developed a lean over the years and took the cottage with it. The same problem has plagued the Hogg cottage.

The lot east of the Flock cottage was kept as pasture until 1924 when it was sold to the **Bremer** family who planned to build a cottage there. That summer they camped on the lot until one tragic Sunday night. The two daughters had taken their grandmother by canoe to the evening service at Christ Church. On the way back just west of Rocky Island, the canoe overturned and the grandmother was

82

drowned. The whole community was in shock as they stood on the town dock watching her body being brought in. The Bremers were so upset that they never returned to the lake. The lot was sold back to Arthur Flock.

The Rogers Cottage

The Rogers family who emigrated from England in 1832 settled in Collingwood where they operated a farm and sold books. Their son, William, attended high school in Barrie before he went to Trinity College where he studied mathematics. After that he became a mathematics teacher at Riverdale Collegiate. It was during his teaching career that he met Arthur Flock and heard the stories about Mary Lake. In 1920 he visited Port Sydney to see this beautiful lake for himself. That summer he and his family (Ted, Rolph, Selby and wife Lillian) stayed with the MacInnes Family in the big house at the corner of Morgan Street and Muskoka Rd.10. The lake was everything that Flock had told them and more.

Ted,Rolph,Selby(on Lap) William and Lillian Rogers (L-R)

In 1921 William bought the second lot east of Arthur Flock's land from William Thoms for $200 a foot. His cottage was a packaged kit that they bought in Barrie from his brother who had a lumber mill. In 1922 it was hauled in from the train in Utterson. The last part of the trip must have been really difficult since there was only a cart track over the hills to the lot. The cottage had three bedrooms, a living room and kitchen. The beautiful fireplace was built by Mr.MacFarlane who did the stone work at Bigwin Inn. William Rogers passed away in 1930 but his wife Lillian continued to come to the lake. Later she added a veranda and in 1946 the cottage was passed on to their son Ted.

Rogers Cottage c 1922

During the summers the family loved to escape the city's heat and relax up here. In early days the road was paved to Bradford but after that it was gravel and often in poor shape. The car would be loaded with supplies for the summer including sides of bacon. In those days cars needed regular stops to top up the water in the radiator.

George Johnson (above) said they would allow two days for the trip from Port Dover in the early 1920's.. They towed a camper trailer behind their car (from the photos, the car was likely a model-T Ford.) and would camp at the property of a family friend near Toronto at the end of the first day. He and a nanny would sleep in the camper-trailer, while his mother and father would share a tent. Highway 2 was the only Macadamized (paved) road on the route. Road maps and signage along the way were provided by the recently-formed Ontario Motor League. George said they could count on at least one flat tire during the course of the journey!

There were always problems in keeping the food cool. They would have ice cut by Dick Thoms in the winter and stored under sawdust in an icehouse. It was the chore of the children to wash off the blocks. They did not get hydro until after WW2.

Uncle William, Bill (Selby)Ted, arriving at cottage

It was a twenty minute row to Port Sydney for supplies and while the parents were shopping William's son, Ted and his brother would swim off the town dock. In those days there was a shed at the end of the dock to store goods from the steamers. It was the height of daring to jump off the top of the shed into the water with local kids like Mel and Bill Clarke.

Town Dock Seen on Regatta Day

William Rogers was a good friend of the Anglican ministers including Rev. Hunt and Canon Pinnington. Canon Pinnington had been a padre in WW 1 and after he returned he became a moving force in Port Sydney. Among other things he is remembered for starting the rifle club that used a range just west of Pine Lodge. On Saturday afternoons the men and women of the village would compete. The prizes were coffee cups.

Canon Pinnington and Captain Ralph Lee of the Muskoka Navigation Company and the Sagamo in the background.

Arthur Flock and William Rogers had another colleague who lived across the lake. Elizabeth Jackson was also a teacher at Riverside Collegiate. She had inherited the family farmhouse at the mouth of Jackson Creek near where Muskoka Lodge was located. In the late 1920's on land north of the creek along what is now Edgemere road she built a nine hole golf course. This became the destination for the men of the community whenever they had some spare time. In those days golf was mainly a male sport.

The Hogg Cottage

The third in this cluster of cottages and the furthest from the head of the bay was the Hogg Cottage. The story starts with Carol Stanton who built the cottage. She was born in 1898 as a student of Arthur Flock at Riverdale Collegiate, once again his stories of the beauty of Mary Lake drew her here. The Stantons had originally come from England in 1642 and settled in the United States where they stayed until 1794 when they moved to Cobourg. Carol had worked in a munitions factory next to the Don Jail during WW1. After the war she attended university. This was unusual in those days when only 6% of women went on to higher education.

She first came to Mary Lake in 1922 and camped near the lake. Apparently it was all that Flock said and more because she bought a fifty foot lot from Dick Thoms that year. She must have been quite adventurous because she also had a small cottage built and an icehouse at the rear. In those days women did not do all these things.

The Hogg Cottage

It was in 1926 that she met and married David Hogg while they were both working at Simpsons. Once again those were different times. Because they were married, she had to leave her work at the store since a married couple could not work at the same location. They spent their honeymoon at the cabin in November that year. David had to build a toboggan to haul their belongings out to the train at the end of the honeymoon. The Hoggs had come from Scotland and his father had been a medical missionary in China before he returned to Canada.

In the 1930's they would take the train to Utterson with their summer supplies. A farmer would transport them to the Thom's farmhouse in a model T. There they would load their belongings into a rowboat for the trip to the cabin. A lot of the summer time was spent in cutting and chopping wood for the winter. Seeing the occasional boat and steamer going past was a special event. Socializing meant either rowing across the lake or walking around the long trail through the bush to Port Sydney to get to the church or store.

It was always a big event when the Flocks, the Rogers, The Thoms and The Hoggs would get together for the annual bonfire. All the year's collection of drift wood would have been put into a big pile on the beach and they would have a great fire to mark the end the summer.

The Glenokawa Story

The boy could hardly contain himself. School was over for the year and he was about to start out on a great adventure.

It had begun early in the morning when the train left Union Station in Toronto. Other boys had joined him. Some were loud and noisy while many were strangely quiet. He had felt sad for a few minutes when he left his parents on the platform but the many new sights soon overcame his loss. The stink of the smoke from the steam engine filled the car as they clattered through towns with strange sounding names. The one that he had watched for was Utterson. It was the stop where he got off to go to Port Sydney. The entrance to Port Sydney was at Mary Lake Motors where all the signs were located. There were over a dozen of them pointing to lodges and camps....but the one he wanted was "Camp Glenokawa"

Signs at Mary Lake Motors

At the town dock he and the others had waited impatiently until the boat ferry came. Jerry Ashton in a peaked hat was the driver. He collected the 25-cent fare for the ride over to the camp which could barely be seen to their left at the head of Echo Bay.

The welcome was tumultuous as the other campers and the camp director Glen Allen, rushed down to the dock to welcome the new boys.

Glen Allen was a pianist, an artist, an actor, a dancer and a conversationalist. He always seemed to be acting. He was larger than life and charmed everyone in his conversations. Glen had been born in 1904 and had joined the famous Dumbell Troup after WW 1 in 1928 during a revival of the troupe in England. For many soldiers in the trenches in the deadly mud of the war, the Dumbell Troupe had been a bright moment of laughter and song as they made fun of army life, did ribald female impersonations and sang risqué songs. For most of his life he used his stage name 'Glen Allen' instead of his real name Arnold Armstrong.

After working at Pinecrest Camp in Bala in 1931, Glen decided to bring his energy and enthusiasm to his own camp for boys on Mary Lake in 1932. He was lucky in getting 30 acres of inexpensive land southwest of Buckhorn Point and a pile of lumber on the town dock left over from a defaulted delivery...and so Camp Glenokawa was born. From then until its demise in 1958 due to competition, hundreds of boys came to the camp mostly for two weeks to learn canoeing, canoe tripping, swimming, archery, boxing, arts and drama. They lived eight to a cabin with no hydro, no phone or road to the camp...and in the main loved it. Glen who was very liberal for the day gave them talks on Sunday nights about the Golden Rules, table manners, sex and held debates about God. He was a character good at drawing kids out by helping shy kids to be heroes and brash kids to tone it down. The graduates of the camp in many cases went on to become successful leaders. One became the director of the National Art Gallery.

The highlight of each summer was the holiday at the beginning of August. The whole camp went into training for the regatta and competitions against their arch- rivals at Pioneer Camp. Because of their emphasis on canoeing, Glenokawa was usually able to clean up on canoeing events. The other big event on that weekend was the show at the community hall. Tickets for seats at the community hall would all be sold out for the show called "The Annual Riot" because this was also a big event for Port Sydney. Glen would spend the winter writing the script for the review and the whole camp would spend over two weeks preparing for this event held on August 1. Props would be prepared that would cover the whole wall at the stage end of the hall. They were painted in sections and glued together. Often there were several of these large sheets. One would be torn down revealing the next one to prepare for the next scene. The crowd loved the presentation which was like the original Dumbell shows. The campers would sing, dance, do impersonations and tell slightly off colour jokes. Parents who came to the shows were sometimes not too impressed with the jokes that their sons were telling.

People in Port Sydney still remember the shows and the camp. Every night the villagers heard the trumpet at the camp playing "taps".

During the years that the camp operated, Glen decorated Eaton's windows in the winter and wrote romance novels. After the camp closing in 1958, Glen was devastated. He went to Denmark only to return in the early 60's broke and in poor health. The boys from the camp came to his rescue and held a reunion. One of the favourite songs at the camp had been " We ain't got a barrel of money" and so they gave him a barrel of money and helped him until his death from cancer in 1978.

The "boy" and his fellow campers still return occasionally to revisit the site of their memories and to look at the two falling down cabins. It is said that sometimes at dusk taps can be faintly heard from Echo Bay.

Not long ago, a woman stood for several minutes at the end of the dock in front of Glenokawa. Her husband who had died recently had been a camper at Glenokawa many years ago. She dropped her wedding ring into the lake thus fulfilling a promise made to him before he died. His fondest memories had been at the camp and his marriage to her. This was the way to bring these special times and memories back together .

Pitman's Bay north of Thoms Bay

Where the name Pitman comes from remains a mystery. It has been suggested that since a family named Petman owned the land in 1886 it may be a misspelled version of that name. By the 1930's it was owned by the Bain family. George Bain died in 1921 but his wife and children camped on the property in the summers during the 1930's and she took in washing to help with the costs.

In 1945 it was learned that the property was going to be sold. Rather than let it end up being used for more cottages, George Hutcheson, Claude Wardell and Sid Avery decided to buy it to be used by the youth of North Muskoka for camping. The cost was $2500. From 1945 until 1951 it became a summer camp for various youth groups and church groups as a summer camp. Mrs. Bain continued as camp cook. In 1951 the Town of Huntsville purchased the 63 acres for $2000. The purchase was in trust for the boy scouts and youth of the Huntsville area. In 1964 the scouts purchased another 50 acres north of the original land to protect it from further development.

In the late 1980's the scouts had to give up the land to the Town of Huntsville because of the problems of assuring that user groups had liability insurance.

It would remain for the use of our youth. **Appendix Seven** is the agreement that is in place with the Town of Huntsville.

Port Sydney Becomes a Town

By the early 1930's life in Port Sydney had become differed considerably from that of the rest of Stephenson Township and yet the township governed the Town. Dissatisfaction with the priorities of the township grew in Port Sydney and the township was unhappy with the pressure that the town tried to exercise over the predominately rural issues of the township. This became evident in a rivalry that developed between Port Sydney and Utterson. By now a large summer population was also putting pressure for change on the local leaders in the town. They were particularly concerned over the condition of the roads.

Clyffe House Hill c 1922

The result was the creation of a local council and the passing of the Port Sydney Act by the provincial government creating the Village of Port Sydney in 1933. The boundaries of the village were: just north of Buckhorn Point on the north, just east of Hawkes Road on the east, just south of Bridgedale and near Ladell's Road on the west. The first village council is seen below and included from left to right: Hugh MacInnes, Mel Clarke, Bob Jenner, Bill Watson and Alex Hughes.

The first village council

Hugh MacInnes He was the son of Alan MacInnes mentioned earlier. At various times he ran the ice cream parlor at Hoth's store, raised and sold flowers, worked for the lumber companies in the winter and he managed the Mary Lake Lunch at the corner of Morgan and Muskoka Rd. 10 for many years.

Mel Clarke: Mel was the grandson of William Clarke and son of Arthur Clarke. Mel continued the family tradition of construction just as his son Richard does today. Mel was a community leader in sports as was mentioned earlier.

Bob Jenner: Bob operated Clyffe House and showed a lot of initiative there and in the community. He built the front part of Clyffe House and built the first concrete tennis courts in the area. He even built a toboggan run south of Muskoka Rd. 10. Typically when he saw how easy it would be for the village kids to slide off the dam as they went to school, he put up a fence and covered the stairs down to the dam.

Bill Watson: He continued the occupation of his dad, Adam Watson and ran the village store for many years. At one time he operated cabins on the large flat land just south of the dam. In 1933 he married a school teacher named Clara, who became a well known villager in her own right.

Alex Hughes He was a plumber and builder in the community who did work for many cottagers as well as Clyffe House.

This was the group that took over local government in 1933 during the depression. It was a time of great privation for the community since jobs had all but disappeared. The council looked after roads, provided money to the local school board which ran SS# 9 just east of the bridge and were to start the local fire department just after the war. One piece of work that they initiated that can still be seen is the line of pine trees that stretches along the road as people come into the town from the west. For years this stretch of road was drifted with snow during the winter. Snow would blow across the open fields and fill up this road. In 1933 a line of pine trees was planted along both sides of the road to block the drifting. They have become a beautiful promenade leading to the town.

The Depression
The cottagers continued to come to Mary Lake in the summer. Many of them had their own financial problems and therefore did not spend much money getting work done thus generating jobs at their cottages.

By 1938 the cottagers around the local lakes had created their own organization called "North Muskoka Lakes Association" which included about 250 members from the chain of lakes and 51 from Mary Lake. The yearbook that year has a number of ads, an elaborate constitution, helpful suggestions, rules of the road, game laws, golf course ads and hours for worship at various churches. That year their main activity was to organize a regatta for all the lakes. Previously the regatta had been held mainly for Peninsula Lake.

Peninsula Lake, Continued:—

Wook, W. H.	34 St. Germaine Ave., Toronto	Penlake P. O.
Wroxhall, Miss E	North James Ave., Avalon, Pa.	Penlake P. O.
Wyndham, Mr. Max	Dundas St., Oakville, Ont.	Penlake P. O.
Wyndham, Mrs. Max	Dundas St., Oakville, Ont.	Penlake P. O.
Wilson, W. J.	3x5 Willard Ave., Toronto	N Portage

FAIRY LAKE

Bartlett, W. G.	53 Appleton Ave., Toronto	Huntsville P. O.
Bartlett, Mrs. W. G.	53 Appleton Ave., Toronto	Huntsville P. O.
Day, Rowland	5 Thornton Ave., Toronto	Fairyport. Huntsville
Eccleston, Mrs. E. J.	39 Vesta Drive, Toronto	Fairyport. Huntsville
Firth, L. M.	240 Russel Hill Rd., Toronto	Huntsville P. O.
Hart, Miss C. G.	1122 Bishop Rd., Grosse Pt., Mich.	Fairyport, Huntsville
Kilmer, T. B.	87 Rivercourt Blvd., Toronto	Huntsville P. O.
Meyers, Miss M.	249 Russell Hill Rd., Toronto	Huntsville P. O.
Monkhouse, C. A.	5x Glen Elm Ave., Toronto	Fairyport, Huntsville
Monkhouse, Mrs. C. A.	53 Glen Elm Ave., Toronto	Fairyport. Huntsville
O'Callahan, F.	1 Salton St., Toronto	Huntsville P. O.
O'Callahan, Mrs. F	1 Salton St., Toronto	Huntsville P. O.
Plunkett, T. S.	118 Lauder Ave., Toronto	Huntsville P. O.
Rogers, Ed.	16 Southgate St., London, Ont.	Fairyport, Huntsville
Verner, R. G.	Grosse Point Park, Mich.	Fairyport, Huntsville
Verner, Mrs Edna	Grosse Point Park, Mich.	Fairyport, Huntsville
Wilson, Mrs. Robt.	50 Pearl St. N., Hamilton, Ont.	Fairyport, Huntsville

MARY LAKE

Bell, Miss K. H.	116 Beech Ave., Toronto	Port Sydney
Clarke, Mrs. Lewis	Port Sydney P. O., Ont.	Port Sydney
Demsick, Miss Amy	600 S. Lafayette, Royal Oak, Mich.	Port Sydney
Demsick, Miss Hellen	608 S. Lafayette, Royal Oak, Mich.	Port Sydney
Duzin Estate	Frances, Ont.	Port Sydney
Doran, W. W.	67 Glenview Ave., Toronto	Port Sydney
Doran, Miss D.	67 Glenview Ave., Toronto	Port Sydney
Fellowes, Mrs. E. L.	Port Sydney P. O. Ont.	Port Sydney
Holmes, Mrs. E. W.	25 Summerhill Ave., Toronto	Port Sydney
Holmes, Dr. Geo.	25 Summerhill Ave., Toronto	Port Sydney
Huth, M. W.	Fairy Sydney P. O., Ont.	Port Sydney
Jackson, Mrs. D. O.	507 Dovercourt Rd., Toronto	Port Sydney
Jackson, Miss E.	507 Dovercourt Rd., Toronto	Port Sydney
Johnson, Rev. H. J.	The Rectory, Alvinston, Ont.	Port Sydney
Johnson, S. M.	Toronto	Port Sydney
Milburd, Mrs. Ella	600 S. Lafayette, Royal Oak, Mich.	Port Sydney
Moodie, C. W.	182 Hughson St. S., Hamilton, Ont.	Port Sydney
Moodie, Mrs. C. W.	182 Hughson St. S., Hamilton, Ont.	Port Sydney
Moodie, Miss Jean	182 Hughson St. S., Hamilton, Ont.	Port Sydney
McClure, P. M.	Port Sydney P. O., Ont.	Port Sydney
McMahon, Dr. C. F.	3410 Cambridge Rd., Detroit, Mich.	Port Sydney
McMahon, Mrs. C. F.	3410 Cambridge Rd., Detroit, Mich.	Port Sydney
McMahon, Miss D. M.	3410 Cambridge Rd., Detroit, Mich.	Port Sydney
Newton, Miss Ivy L. G.	33 Erindale Ave., Toronto	Port Sydney
Raloff, Mrs. Rosa J.	17017 Scottsdale Blvd., Shaker Heights, Cleveland, Ohio	Port Sydney
Smith, Master H. A.	03 Wells St., Toronto	Port Sydney

Mary Lake, Continued:—

Sutherland, J. E.	Port Sydney, Ont.	Port Sydney
Sutherland, Miss Siddie	182 Hughson St. S., Hamilton, Ont.	Port Sydney
Vipond, Miss A. D.	16 "The Oaks", Bain Ave., Toronto	Port Sydney
Walker, A. M.	49 Prospect Ave. S., Hamilton	Port Sydney
Wright, Mrs. Emily A.	21 Robina Ave., Toronto	Port Sydney
Wright, Miss Dorothy	21 Robina Ave., Toronto	Port Sydney
HUNTSVILLE		
J. R. Boyd and Son	Huntsville, Ont.	Huntsville, Ont.
Fraser, Mr. John G.	Huntsville, Ont.	Huntsville, P. O.
Rice, Mr. H. E.	Huntsville, Ont.	Huntsville, P. O.
Rice, Mr. F. N.	Huntsville, Ont.	Huntsville, P. O.
McTaggart, Rev. Hugh	Huntsville, Ont.	Huntsville P. O.
Constable, R. F.	Huntsville	Huntsville
VERNON LAKE		
Cavan, Margaret	87 Lansdale Road, Toronto, Ont.	Camp Onawaw, via Huntsville

* Deceased.

There were many local problems during the depression. Men who had jobs in the city were laid off and returned to the village. There they planted big gardens hoping for the revival of the economy. There were just no local jobs. Some of the young men went north to the mines in Kirkland Lake. Bill Clarke, grandson of William and son of Lewis played intermediate hockey in Kirkland Lake and was given a job in the mines. C.W Moodie had a large number of shares in The Lakeshore Mining Company there and managed to get jobs for some of the young men of the village. Others lined up at the gate of the mine each morning hoping that they would get called up from the waiting crowd to work in the mines that day.

The depression was a sad way to end the two decades after WW1. The mood in the community had been really optimistic after the war. Together with the newcomer cottagers, the local community had become a far different place than had existed before the war. Even though the community survived the depression, it must have been a dreary prospect when people had to face the dark clouds of the coming war looming at the end of the 1930's .

Conclusion

The story of Port Sydney during its first 70 years is about the waves of newcomers and their changing attitudes about their surroundings.. From the first settlers confronted by the daunting rock and forest landscape, to the tourists brought to the area by its spectacular beauty, to the returning soldiers who saw all kinds of new possibilities in their surroundings and finally to the cottagers and campers, each group of newcomers found ways to capitalize on the potential of the area. Initially they found ways to make an income from the trees and later to see ways to live in harmony with the environment that enhanced their lives. They initiated the attitudes about conserving their environment that still exist today.

Recently the community advanced to the final stage of this process started in the 1870's: people against nature, people capitalizing on their environment, people admiring their environment, people living in harmony with their environment and finally people protecting their environment. The community, through the Mary Lake Association wrote the Mary Lake Plan for inclusion in the Official Plan of Huntsville. It expresses the views of the community that have developed from these foundations. **See Appendix Eight**

The other day I stood among these newcomers in the cemetery…familiar names on headstones around me. Their toil and struggle is long behind them. It was a soft summer day and birds flitted from tree to tree. I lingered around the tombstones under that benign sky. Nearby the waves lapped on the shoreline and a seagull wheeled above. Now these newcomers sleep in that quiet soil beside the lake.

Newcomers to Port Sydney today are awed by the beauty and presence of the lake, the islands and the hills. There are few communities in Ontario where the panorama is so impressive. The charm of the community and the success of its citizens lies in how they have adapted and changed their perception towards this setting in the years since 1870. May they continue to cherish our surroundings.

Appendices

Appendix One
The Muskoka Road Opened for Settlement
[Canada, Department of Crown Lands, Report, 1859, pp.18, 74-75]

.... The Muskoka Road leading from Lake Simcoe to High Falls on the River Muskoka was opened for settlement during the past year, and in the month of August last Mr. Jos. Oliver was appointed resident agent. He has reported 54 locations. Most of the locatees have taken possession of their lots, and have built shanties and made small clearings. The lands on this road are not generally of so good a quality as on the other Settlement Roads, but they are easily accessible by the Northern Railway and steamer on Lake Simcoe, and the road itself was undertaken and has been completed as a most important means of communication, - leading as it does from the head of the navigable waters of Lake Simcoe into the interior of the country, and meeting the great leading road now nearly completed, which connects the River Ottawa at Farrell's Point with The Georgian Bay....

Crown Land Department
    P.M Vankoughnet
Quebec, February 28, 1860
    Commissioner

Muskoka and Haliburton 1615 -1875
A Collection of Documents
Florence B. Murray
U of T Press 1963

Appendix Two
A Traveller on The Muskoka Road
Mrs. King, Letters from Muskoka by an Emigrant Lady, pp 24-29

....We landed at Washago, and after standing for more than an hour on the quay, took the stage wagon for Gravenhurst, the vehicle being so crowded that even the personal baggage most essential to our comfort had to be left behind. Oh! The horrors of that journey! The road was most dreadful...our first acquaintance with "corduroy" roads. The forest gradually closed in on us, on fire on both sides, burnt trees crashing down in all directions, here and there one right across the road, which had to be dragged out of the way before we could go on. Your brother with his arm around me the whole way (I clinging to the collar of his coat), could hardly keep me steady as we bumped over every obstacle. In the worst places I was glad to shut my eyes that I might not see the danger. Your poor sister had to cling convulsively to the rope which secured the passenger's baggage (ours was left behind and we did not see it for weeks) to avoid being thrown out, and for long afterwards we both suffered from the bruises we received and the strain upon our limbs. At last, long after dark, we arrived at Gravenhurst, where we were obliged to sleep, as the steamer for Bracebridge could not start before morning on account of the fog. The steamboat had no accommodation for sleeping, but we had a good supper on board, and a gentlemanly Englishman, a passenger by the stage and well acquainted with Muskoka, took us to a small hotel to sleep. The next morning we went to Bracebridge.....

The drive from Bracebridge to Utterson, the nearest post-town to our settlement and distant from it six miles, was a long and fatiguing stretch of fifteen miles, but unmarked by any incident of consequence. The forest fires were burning fiercely, and our driver told us that a week before the road had been impassible. At times when the trees were burning at each side of the narrow road we felt a hot stifling air as we passed rapidly along. It was a gloomy afternoon, with fitful gusts of wind portending a change in weather, and we were almost smothered in clouds of Muskoka dust, much resembling pounded bricks. When we got to Utterson we were obliged to remain for two hours to rest the poor horses, as no fresh ones were to be got........

Muskoka and Haliburton 1615 -1875
A Collection of Documents
Florence B. Murray
U of T Press 1963

Appendix Three

October 4, 1869.

My dear Mrs. Hands,

I have no doubt you were surprised to receive my letter before we left Birmingham. Still what has been done I trust will be for the best and I think it will be.

We left Liverpool on the 9th of September by the ship **MORAVIAN***, a Clyde built steamer and 300 feet in length worth ^100,000 and capable of accommodating more than a thousand passengers. The scene going on board is indescribable - everything was confusion. Now I will give you a few particulars concerning our voyage across the Atlantic.*

***THURSDAY SEPT. 9th** - We sailed at 2 p.m. Weather fine. We did not feel sick at all the first few hours. We were on deck all afternoon and enjoyed it very much. Towards 5 o'clock Mother went below. She said she did not feel so well as when she started. Soon after she came up again and asked me why I did not come to my tea. I went with her downstairs and looked at the tea and that was quite sufficient for me. All round the table where the tea was laid people were sitting with their basins on their laps as sick as possible. So you may think it would not have been very pleasant to have sat down to my tea there. I went to Mother again who was sick three times so she went to her berth. She said I had*

106

better come too, so I got into bed and lay there for an hour when I thought I had better get out and undress for the night. I did not feel at all sick but my head felt very strange and then I fainted. I hurt my head falling against the corner of one of the berths. They were very kind to us and made me a bed where I could get some fresh air and when I felt better carried me back to my berth. It was caused by the closeness of the place where the berths are very small. When I got back to my berth I was sick so felt better. We undressed and went into our berths again. About 3 a.m. we were woke by the pitching and tossing of the vessel. The waves washed right over the deck. It is in more than 28 fathoms of water. The noise below was something awful and at the same time very distressing. People retching and groaning enough to make anyone feel bad.

FRIDAY SEPT. 10ᵗʰ *- We got up at quarter to six, dressed and went on deck. It was very windy and the sea was very rough. We are now in sight of Lough Foyle and the Irish coast and are to remain here until 5 p.m. when the mails and a few more passengers come aboard. Last night while the vessel was rolling the beam on which the men's hammocks swing gave way and let six of them down on the floor. We stayed on deck all day. At 7 p.m. they advised us to go below to our berths. They said in half an hour from then the decks would be covered with water; and so they were. Heavy seas kept breaking over her all night.*

SATURDAY SEPT. 11th *- We are out on the open sea now. We had a pretty good night and got up at 6:00 a.m. As long as we were in our berths we were alright, but as soon as we got out we began to feel sick again. We got upstairs and sat between decks for a while. Mother was very bad with diarrhea and had to see the Doctor. We were both very sick but after a time we were helped on deck where we lay the whole of the day not being able to taste anything and feeling very bad indeed. At 12 a.m. today we were 311 miles from Liverpool making 10 knots an hour. The wind is against us. We went below at 7 p.m. and tumbled into our berths just as we were.*

SUNDAY SEPT. 12th *- We had a very rough night and did not get up till 7 a.m. We went between decks but could not get any farther as the deck was wet. We sat down and were sick three times. Then after a while they helped us on deck again where we had another day not being able to walk or eat either. Pleasant! Everyone is kind to us. They will do anything for us. There is not to be any service today because the passengers are too ill to attend. It does not seem like Sunday at all - so different to our peaceful Sabbaths in Birmingham. It has been very fine all afternoon but rough and now the moon is shining on the waters. It is* *a beautiful night. We feel better tonight and are now just going to bed. It is now 8 o'clock.*

MONDAY SEPT. 13th - *We got up soon after six and managed to get on deck but it was so rough we could scarcely keep on our feet. One minute we think we are going to be pitched forward over the one side and the next we think we are going to be sent flying over the other side. We are pretty well today and begin to fancy we should take something tasty to eat, not having tasted anything since Friday. We have been living on Sea Air. I can assure you we get plenty tossing about on this vast Atlantic Ocean. Tonight the Steward brought us a nice piece of beef steak. He said it would do us good. The food you have given you is very good and wholesome but after you have been sick you feel you want something nice.*

TUESDAY SEPT. 14th - *Last night we went to our berths at 7:30 as the sea was very rough. We woke at half past one. The sea was fearfully rough. We thought every minute the ship would turn right over. We woke at 8 a.m. This morning we cannot rest below but get on deck as soon as we are able. We have seen a few seagulls today. Quite a treat to see something besides the ship. At 6 bells (11 o'clock) today there was a whale seen. You may guess we are nearing the colder regions. We have only 1100 miles to go now. They have got all the sails out today and we are going along faster. It is such fun. Now we are better we try to walk across the decks. We have to cling to ropes or whatever comes in our way and nine times out of ten you slip. The wind is so strong it takes us off our feet. The Stewards are the kindest men. Just now we got a nice slice of Plum Pudding and a piece of Suckling pig. We never touch anything now provided for the Steerage Passengers.*

WEDNESDAY SEPT. 15th - *Yesterday we went over 300 miles. It seems a long distance. It rained all afternoon so I went and sat "tween decks" with my knitting till it was time to go below. Mother is very bad again today with diarrhea. I am alright now. We are sitting downstairs today for it is bitter cold on deck.*

THURSDAY SEPT. 16th - *Yesterday we went over 316 miles. The wind has been very favourable the last few days. It is a very fine day and much warmer. I can do without my shawl today. The ship does not roll so much either and the sun shines brightly on the beautiful water. I went on deck till half past seven. It was a glorious moonlight night.*

FRIDAY SEPT. 17th - *Last night there was a squall. I did not know anything about it till I got up this morning. It seems Mother had been awake and heard it and had been very much frightened by it. For three hours in the night the ship went at the rate of 18 miles an hour - such a rate she never went at before. They sighted Newfoundland early this morning and we are going on deck to see it. There is Labrador on the one side and Newfoundland on the other. A gentleman lent me his glass and we saw three icebergs. They did glitter in the sun. There was also a beautiful white lighthouse to be seen on the shore on the one side of us. The land looked nothing but a broad black line, but Labrador looked beautiful and bright in parts, in others dark and rugged. It is one of the most glorious days we have had yet. The water is as calm as a millpond and when the sun shines upon it it glistens like so many diamonds. Everyone is in excellent spirits. The sight of land seems to have revived us all. I forgot to say there were more than 670 passengers aboard. We were up by 5 o'clock this morning. It seems so funny that at 5 a.m. here it is 9 a.m. in England. Mother was very bad in the night, but she is bright enough today. We have just seen a shoal of porpoises. The river is alive with them. There were thousands and thousands of them. They jump right out of the water and then dart down again. Soon after that we saw a great many divers. They fly about and then dive down in the water after the fish. They are about the size of pigeons.*

At 6 o'clock we went between decks and saw the sailors dancing Hornpipes, etc. I am quite sure some of these sailors would shame many of our fine young men at Balls or Parties in town. They dance light and graceful.

At half past seven we came on deck again. The moon was shining on the beautiful water. It is indeed a glorious sight to see the moon shining on the peaceful waters. The sky was very red and the reflection on the water was lovely. How I wish you and Mrs. Cresswell could have seen it. It would have done your heart good to have seen it. At nine o'clock we went to bed. It seemed a sin to leave the lovely moonlight. I could not go to sleep but lay awake the whole of the night. Every half hour I heard them strike the bell and cry "All's well".

SATURDAY SEPT. 18th - *We got up at 5 o'clock, washed and went on deck. it was cold but pleasant. The water is still smooth and at times scarcely a ripple to be seen. We are sailing along the great river St. Lawrence now. It is a noble looking river and abounds in fish. On the shores we can see the limestone* cliffs and pine forests, and here and there villages that look like white specks in the distance. Yesterday we went over 323 miles and we have only about 350 miles or so to go. If all goes well we shall see Quebec tomorrow.

We have seen about a dozen ships today. They took so pretty in the distance. The sunset this evening is indeed lovely. I wish I could describe it as I ought, but I cannot. In one part there is every shade of green, and in others it looks as if the sky were a blazing fire. The reflection on the water is something beautiful. To stand by the side of the ship and look first on the water and then at the sky and lovely scenery on each side of the river seems to fill your heart with gratitude to Him who gave us sight and sense to enjoy the beauties He has created. I do not think anyone can really feel how great God is till they see some of the mighty wonders He has wrought. Mother has not been on deck so much today. She has been with Mrs. Owens, who I must tell you has been one of our kindest friends on board.

SUNDAY SEPT. 19th - This morning at 2:20 a.m. we had to turn back. There was a thick fog and we had missed the place where the pilot had to come aboard. They fired twice and was answered the second time. They were firing rockets throughout the night as signals. It is dangerous to be so near land and in a fog too. Mother got up as soon as the cannon went of and I got up about half past three. We could not sleep. We walked about below until about half past four when we went on deck. It was still very foggy. At 9 a.m. it cleared and was very fine though windy. The scenery on each side was beautiful. The pine forests, and here and there a maple tree with its red leaves. The farms, too, are neatly laid out and a few churches scattered about. At half past ten we had service in the Saloon. I stood most of the afternoon looking at the scenery. At half past two we saw the Falls of Montmorency and two hours after we arrived at Quebec. We did not land on the Quebec side of the river. We landed at Point Levy. We did not leave the boat till half past seven. It took all that time to get the luggage out, and it so happened that our boxes did not come out with the first.

Through the kindness of a gentleman on board all our boxes were passed and marked by the Custom House Officer without opening one of them. We then went and had tea and from there we went to the station. It was 8 o'clock. We waited there till half past one in the morning before the train started. When we got to the station at first they told us the train might start in an hour or it might be two or three hours. They could not tell till the luggage train had gone. The trains here are very convenient. You can walk from one to the other. We had a fearful storm of thunder and lightening which lasted a few hours.

110

MONDAY SEPT. 20th - *We arrived in Montreal at half past three today after traveling 180 miles from Point Levis here. After we had washed and taken tea we went to see Jim [a brother] . We have just arrived in time as he leaves here the day after tomorrow for New York and from there he goes to New Orleans. When we got to where he is staying we were told that Will [another brother] was there waiting for us. He has been very ill, but is quite well now. His illness was brought on by excessive vomiting. He vomited a whole week coming across from England to the States. He was in the hospital 157 days and only left in time to meet us at Montreal. He was well taken care of and had everything that was nourishing - Port every day at 12 o'clock and if he felt low he had whiskey given him. His illness had been long and serious. Several times his life was despaired of but thank God he is quite well now and we do not intend to lose him again.*

Jim sent him money to bring him over a thousand miles to Montreal. Will had a fearful passage out. The bulwarks were stove in, six buckets carried overboard and the ship dreadfully knocked about. He said he never expected to see land again.

TUESDAY SEPT. 21st -*We went with Jim to see the French Cathedral of Notre Dame. It is a noble looking place. The inside is gorgeous in the extreme - stained glass windows, etc. I could not describe it or I would. From there we went to see the Jesuit Church. I thought Notre Dame was a fine place, but the Jesuit Church is grand and far surpasses the other. Some altars with candles all round and flowers in abundance. There are pictures all round illustrating the life of Christ.*

We intended to go round the town but could not on account of the rain. At half past seven we left Montreal for Toronto. We had to say "Goodbye" to Jim here. He has got a long journey, over 4000 miles, all by train.

These Canadian cars are dreadful things for shaking, but I suppose it is the rough roads that cause that. This is certainty a most beautiful country. Our route lay through forest, hills, over rivers and lakes. Lake Ontario is the largest I have seen.

We arrived at Toronto at half past one a.m. having traveled 330 miles more. After we had dined we went out and looked at the town. The streets are lined on each side with trees. The pavements are wood and took clean and are very nice to walk on. The greatest nuisance is the flies.

THURSDAY SEPT. 23rd - *We left the place we had stayed at and went to the station, about a mile distant, and got there at half past six a.m. As I lay in bed last night I had a fine view of Lake Ontario, or I should say part of it for it is 300 miles in length.*

*At 7 a.m. the train left Toronto. At half past eight we had a narrow escape. They just had time to get our train on to another line when a luggage train came down on the very line we had just come up. We arrived at Bell Ewart at 10 o'clock. Then we walked down the pier to the Steamer **EMILY MAY** to cross Lake Simcoe.*

*It is indeed worth coming across and enduring hardships if only to see the grand and beautiful scenery. We go to Orillia by this steamer and shall be on the water about five hours. We arrived at Orillia at quarter past two; then we had to cross a narrow landing stage to where the little tug **CARRIELLA** was waiting to convey us to Washago, a distance of 12 miles. The scenery was lovely, islands dotted here and there. We got to Washago at 4 o'clock and there we found the stage waiting to take us to Gravenhurst - 15 miles.*

*This is the worst part of the journey. It is over corduroy roads and over great boulders of rock and through partly cleared land. The shaking we got was fearful. The last eight miles lay through thick forests and it was dark too. There is no twilight here, as soon as the sun goes down it is dark. We crossed a bridge over the Kahsheshebogamog River. We arrived at Gravenhurst at 9 a.m. and there we got out of the stage onto the Steamer **WENONAH** that was to take us to Bracebridge, a distance of 16 miles. By this time we were pretty well tired out.*

We had tea on board and then Father, Will, Nellie and I went on deck. It was a splendid moonlight night and the River Muskoka that we were sailing up looked glorious. The trees are hanging over each side. This part of the river is not wider than New Street. I cannot tell you how much we enjoyed it. The Captain came to us and asked us if we were newcomers, and then he gave Father information concerning the land in different parts. He was very kind and last Sunday we met him and he very kindly asked if we were comfortable. We arrived at Bracebridge soon after 11 o'clock p.m. tired and sleepy.

FRIDAY SEPT. 24th - *We got up at six o'clock, had breakfast, and went out a bit. Mother had been very bad again with diarrhea. There are falls within stones throw from where we are staying. Mother is delighted with the place -*

indeed we all are. It is a very healthy place. There are many pretty birds here. Father has shot several and the children have caught a few fish. We have only to cross a field and there is the river. There they can catch as many fish as they want. There are also thousand of black crickets and sawyers.

Father has been very unwell today with the same complaint as Mother. He says all newcomers have it. At 6 o'clock this evening Father and Will started to walk to Stephenson, a distance of 16 miles, to took at the land with two farmers from Stephenson. They will not be back before Monday. The weather is warm and beautiful.

SATURDAY SEPT. 25th - Today we have quite a change in the weather. It is very cold. The people are very kind to us where we are staying but it will not suit the "pocket" to stay here so we are going to rent a small house till Father decides on his land.

SUNDAY SEPT. 26th - We had a sprinkling of snow today. We went to church, there were only 20 persons present.

MONDAY SEPT. 27th - Today it is fine and warm again. We ate in our new house now. Two young men have been keeping Bachelor's Hall this summer here but have kindly gone somewhere else that we might have the place. There is a large stove in and they have given us the use of it free. They are invaluable things, are the stoves. You can boil five pots, a large wash boiler, and bake your bread all at the same time. Unfortunately we cannot get one this winter. They cost too much. They want $30. for them. They are cheap at that, but we cannot afford it. We shall get a three-legged pot and have an open fireplace, put on bread and cover it all over with fire and then let it bake - we shall have to put up with a few inconvenience.

A neighbour kindly lent us her washboard and we washed five dozen clothes in the time it would take to wash two dozen in the old style of rubbing with the hands. You know what a chemist rolls his pills on, well it is like that only on a large scale. We get plenty of milk for nothing. Yesterday one of the farmers killed a cow and today he sent Mother a bit for her breakfast weighing over 10 pounds.

MONDAY OCT. 4th - Father came home last Tuesday (Sept. 28th) from Stephenson. He has got 600 acres of fine land given to him. It is a few acres short of the 600 but what he is short of in land is made up to him in water. There is a

113

lovely river running through our land and we shall have a bridge over it next spring. There are thousands of cherry and nut trees on our land. They gave me 100 acres because I was over 18 years of age. Father has taken up 100 acres for Jim and 100 acres for Bob. Jim will spend his summer with us as every settler is compelled to live six months in every year on his land. Father and Will have gone again to Stephenson to see about getting a house up for us, so I guess we shall only stop here a week of two longer. Still please address:-

Post Office - Bracebridge - Muskoka - Ontario - N.A. until you hear from us again. Nellie and I walked six miles with them and then turned back. We are having glorious weather.

Now dear Mrs. Hands I trust you will not forget us if we are separated by a big pool of water but write a line of two when you can, or if it would not be asking too much will my cousin Fred write to me. We shall be delighted to hear from any of you.

Give out sincere love to Mrs. Cresswell and William. I will write to Mr. C. next. Give out kind regards to Mr. Hands and all enquiring friends, and accept our fondest love yourself and Believe me yours very very sincerely, Anne E. Kay

Post Office

Bracebridge, Muskoka, Ontario, N.A.

Anne's brother Alfred, who was 8 at the time, picks up the story and describes the life of the Kays in their early years in Port Sydney in the book called "Pioneer Days in Port Sydney".

The first snow arrived that year on October 22 but by mid November the family had constructed a cabin 16' x 20'. The cabin had two windows which was a real luxury for the time. The family lived in this house for the first ten years and then moved to a new house a quarter mile up the river. The first house was abandoned because it was behind a hill and was in shadow a lot of the time. They were both called the 'Inverness House' as a memory of their Scottish background. William Kay who was 2 years older than Alfred made the two pencil sketches of the houses about 1885.

114

Appendix Four

Butcher Diary- Mary Caldwell Butcher

1891

Dec 29 A Party at Aspdin tonight

Dec 30 George and I went to Hays after tea to spend the evening. There was quite a party there.

1892

Jan 2 George put out notices for a shooting match. Started a new bag of flour today George opened a potato pit.

Jan 19 the coldest yet 32 below zero. George went to play chess with Mr. Hay.

Jan 30 Mr. and Mrs. Hay moved away today and Mr. Chester is there.

Mar 2 I washed and in the afternoon walked to the Galls Gael

Mar 8 The four Thoms girls came here for tea.

Mar 16 Choir practice here tonight, quite a few came to it.

Mar 21 Mrs.Ladell died this morning leaving a little baby a week old.

April 1 Jokes are flying today. Roads very bad Old Browns burned out. Two dances tonight

April 11 4 eggs today, Magic Lantern at school house to night. George was engaged as night watchman at mill.

May 14 Louisa Gall and Connie and Ruth Thoms came to stay over.

May 17 George took measurements for shingle Mill

May 24 Queen's birthday. Rose bright and fine but rained in the afternoon. We went to the picnic.

115

Nov 10 Thanksgiving Day. A fall of snow last night. I went to church with Sarah and Nelly and enjoyed the service .Came back to dinner of roast goose and George came just in time. The little ones are very good. We had some music in the evening.

1893 Much of 1893 spent in Meaford
1894
Feb 5 Concert at Aspdin tonight

Feb 10 Horrible day cold wind I am reading Vanity Fair in the evenings.

Mar 22 George's birthday 41 He went sawing wood with Mr. Jones.

April 18 Hot day. Terribly destructive fire in Huntsville. Ice gone out of the lake.

May 23 Nice day. Mosquitos are coming in full force tonight like rain. I went to Ladells and saw the Thoms girls.

June 4 We stayed in sewing. Book agent called. Political meeting. George went.

June 29 I baked for the picnic. I went bathing. Connie and Louie rowed over to the Thomses.

July 27 Very hot 97 in the shade. Concert in the hall in aid of the organ fund. There was over $30. made

Sept 4 Sultry. George drove the stage. In the evening George went duck shooting but got nothing. Smoky and very dry.

Sept 21 Mr. Thom Mr. Price and George went shooting and were to dinner and tea. Got 3 partridges.

Oct 8 I cleaned stove and mopped bedroom. Nellie scrubbed bedrooms. Thoms girls came in the evening for Connie.

Oct 17   George is finished night watching at the mill. He is getting subscribers for a daily newspaper.

Oct 27   MacCabe Lodge here tonight . George and party hunted at Clearwater Lake.

Nov 12 George went out still hunting. I had a bad tooth ache. Lou Clarke shot a big deer.

Nov 13 George cut up our pig (weighed 172 pounds) and salted it. Lodge meeting tonight.

Dec 8   Shooting match went off very well. George won a goose. Lodge meeting tonight.

Dec 26 Mr. Rumball died. George went to Utterson to unload a car.

1895

Jan 21   I was taken sick at 12 last night and the baby was born at 1:30 before either Mrs. Brown or Mrs. Forrest who had been sent for arrived. The school house took fire but was put out after considerable damage was done.

Jan 31   George went to a meeting about opening a reading room at the hall.

Feb 14 I went out for the first time. Henry Gall brought a bag of potatoes.

Mar 11 The Thoms girls came and we quilted.

March 22   George's birthday. Oyster supper in the evening.

May 2   Finished papering the dining room and went to Women's Auxiliary meeting

June 27 George got up early and went to Huntsville in Mr. Smith's pretty steamer.

July 12 Mr. Thom and Will Gall came. Steamboat excursion from Huntsville. Connie went to Utterson to see the Orangemen

Sept 3   Warmer we washed. Charlie and Eva are sick. Asked Mr. Clarke to make us a cradle.

Sept 7   Dr.Hart came and said he was afraid that the children were sick with Typhoid

Sept 12 Children rather better. The Dr. came at 1 this morning. The baby was sick all night and I did not sleep much.

Sept 17 Presbyterian Picnic. Dr. came children much better. The well is nearly completed and there is good water.

Oct 11 Wet day. The children are up and dressed but not downstairs yet.

Oct 21 I fumigated and cleaned the sick rooms and moved my bed into the larger room for the winter.

Nov 23 George went to the Jenners and sold them an organ.

Dec 5   A terrible thing happened while we were at the parsonage. Bertie Mitchell broke through the ice skating and was drowned before he could be got out.

Dec 20 Singer Sewing Machine agents came and stayed overnight in the village

1896

April 6 Easter Monday. The three Thoms boys came and spent the day here. I called at the Forrests with the children. Baby has been weaned without any trouble.

April 9   Warm. Henry Gall drove his mother across the lake to see us George went to Utterson.

April 11   I took the children to see the new school.

April 23 We cleaned the bedroom and ironed, Baby and Louie have croup. Had to keep them in. Mr. Hall came to see the sewing machine. George went to Seeleys to see about buying bark.

May 23 Alfred Kay brought Charlie a rabbit. Mr. Leith called about buying an organ. Finished washing and churned.

June 29 Washed and Baked. Got my tooth lanced. George went to the Galls. Piled lumber at the mill. Baked for the picnic.

July 23 George and I went and got about 9 qts of Huckleberries. Laura & Louie Thoms and Mini Forrest came for tea.

August 24   Busy all day. Preserved some plums. George busy sawing wood for winter. I went to the Smiths . had a jolly evening there, quite a crowd there.

Nov 6 Colder. Allan McInnis killed the pig. Mr. Forrest came to arrange a hunt. George went to Utterson for half a day to unload a car. Recipe for pickles…6 lbs of salt,2 oz. of saltpeter, 1 qt. of molasses, 4 gals of water.

Nov 13 George and Mr. Brymer and Lou Clarke went deer hunting and got a nice large one. We got a hind quarter. I finished Eva's coat for school. Tax man came.

Dec 8   Henry Gall bought 94 lbs of beef at 5 cents per lb. George at mill piling kindling wood.

Dec 17 Louie and I went to Ladell's. There was a cheap concert at night. Something over $4. realized .Frozen up. Good skating. Dance at the hall tonight to dance the old year out. I hope the next year will be more prosperous.

Appendix Five
The Town Hall

Port Sydney, Jan. 17th 1921.

Meeting of the Ratepayers of S.S. No 9 Stephenson held at the Home of Mr. McClure on the evening of the above date to discuss the building of a Community Hall

Present – Mr. Bennett; A.W. Clarke Hugh R. Brown; Mr. Stanworth; Mr. Hoth; Mr. R. Jenner; Mr. A. Watson; Rev. A.T. Lowe (Victor Clarke Hugh McInnes; Hubert Brown)

McClure-Watson
That Mr. Lowe be chairman
– Carried

McClure – Stanworth
That Hubert Brown be sec'y
– Carried

Jenner-Stanworth
That Mr. McClure, Mr. Clarke, Mr. Watson and Mr. Brown see

Mr. Smith about a site for the
hall.
                              - Carried

        The size of the hall and the
cost of building it, was discussed
and it was decided, that the hall
should be 30' X 70'; a Two Story building
(~~basement included~~); basement to
be arranged so that there may be
club rooms put in it.

Mr. Stanworth - Mr. G Clarke
        That a limit of $3600 be
put on the estimate for the building
of the hall
                              - Carried

McClure - Hoth
        That this meeting adjourn
until called by the Committee

                A. T. Lowe, Chairman
                Hubert Brown Sec'y

                    121

Port Sydney, Apr. 14th 1921.

Minutes of the meeting of the
Ratepayers of S. S. no 9 Stephenson
held at the home of Mr. McClure
on the evening of the above date.

Present.— Rev. Currie; Mr W. Hoth;
A. G. McInnes; M. McClure; T. Coon;
A. W. Clarke; A. T. Lowe; Rev. Hutton
L. Clarke; R. Jenner. (W. Watson;
V. Clarke; G. Brown; H. McInnes;
H. Brown)

L. Clarke - McClure
That the minutes of the
last meeting be adopted as read.
                        - Carried
The Committees report was
received saying that they had
purchased the Picnic Grounds
from Mr. Smith for the sum of
$800. The money is to be paid
over as soon as the deeds are

ready.   – Carried

    Jenner – L. Clarke
      That we ask Mr. Currie to
give us an approximate estimate
for the building of the hall using his
plan with the stucco walls.
                     – Carried

    McClure – L. Clarke
      That Mrs. A. Clarke, Mrs. McInnes,
and Mrs. Jenner be a committee to
consult with Mr. Currie as to the
details of his plans.
                     – Carried

    Watson – Jenner
      That the funds belonging
to the Cricket Club be handed over
to go toward the purchasing of the
property.   – Carried
      A hearty vote of thanks
was given to the Committee that
interviewed Mr. Smith and to Mrs.
Currie
    Coon – Jenner
      That this meeting adjourn

Appendix Six
Norah Malone Garden's Description of the Interior of Birkswyld (circa 1936)

The kitchen, on the road side of the cottage, was divided by a curtain that could be drawn at mealtimes to separate the room into kitchen and dining room areas. There was a rectangular table with long benches on each side. When guests were present, household tasks were divided to teams of two, one pair doing kitchen duty, while the other pair carried water, cleaned the lamps, tidied and dusted. The next day the pairs switched duties. A filled kettle was kept on the woodstove to supply hot water.

The water tank in the kitchen had a very simple level indicator. On one end of a cord was a heavy nail which hung outside the tank. The cord went through the overflow pipe and on the other end of the cord was a cork which floated on top of the water in the tank. As the water was used, the cork went down and the nail went up. When the nail neared the top it was time for a refill. If an enthusiastic pumper (often a grateful guest) overfilled the tank, water spouted from the overflow pipe! Bystanders often became soaked before the pumper heard the shouts to "stop".

In the centre of the main room was a walnut pedestal table covered by a dark cloth. It had been constructed by their father from wood salvaged from a church fire in Kingston. Above it hung a lamp suspended from the rafters in such a way that it could be lowered for lighting. The lamp was white porcelain decorated with pink roses. Its shade was made of chintz gathered into a series of filigree brass hoops. Crystal pendants hung from the rim. On a side table was a gilded brass lamp with a pump to pressurize the fuel. The base of the lamp was similar to an elaborate trophy.

Two types of cane-bottomed chairs surrounded the central table. A platform rocker faced the small iron stove used for heating. The stove was black with small windows of mica. A dark wooden cupboard held china and glassware. Many little shelves had been fastened between the joists to hold books and knick-knacks. Each of these shelves had a pleated skirt of dark flower-printed fabric hiding the contents of the shelf below. The same fabric had been used to make window curtains, cushions for the chairs and a cover for the oak framed couch. This fabric was a recycled set of drapes. Nothing usable was wasted. Sheets and blankets had been well used before arriving at Birkswyld. They had been turned sides to the middle and darned or patched as required. In those days, thrifty housewives saved all worn out clothes to be bundled and sent to a factory where they were cut into strips and woven into rugs. Birkswyld had quite a few of these.

In each bedroom was a small square table with a floor length pleated skirt tacked around it. Another square piece of the same fabric covered the top. A mirror hung above a small shelf skirted with the same material. Other similar shelves, as well as coat hooks, were on the walls.

Francis had an iron double bed painted white with both the head and foot boards being intricately designed. The brass knobs that should have been on the posts were missing. Her bedroom china was patterned with dark pink roses. Emily had a large mahogany bed with rolled ends and wide strips of wood along the sides. Her bedroom china was white with a gold rim. The two guest rooms were furnished with brown metal beds and plain white china.

The large veranda facing the lake, although screened, was too windy for comfort most of the time. Large green and white striped canvas awnings could be pulled down over the windows and fastened against the wind. There were two old couches on the veranda that could be used for overflow beds. One was an old oak studio couch; the other appeared to be homemade with a straw mattress.

Appendix Seven

MEMORANDUM OF AGREEMENT made in duplicate this seventh day
of December, One thousand nine hundred and fifty-one

FROM CRAIG SMN,

Between

THE CORPORATION OF THE TOWN OF HUNTSVILLE

hereinafter called the Corporation
of the First Part

-and-

HUNTSVILLE BOY SCOUT ASSOCIATION

hereinafter called the Association
of the Second Part.

WHEREAS the Boy Scout Association is presently operating a
summer camp on Lot number twenty-nine (29) in the eighth (8th)
Concession and the southerly fifty (50) acres more or less of
Lot number twenty-nine (29) in the ninth (9th) Concession of
the Township of Stephenson in the District of Muskoka;

AND WHEREAS the said property has been conveyed to The Corporation of the Town of Huntsville and the said Corporation has
agreed to hold the title to the said lands in trust as hereinafter provided:

NOW THIS AGREEMENT WITNESSETH that the said Corporation, for
itself, its successors and assigns, hereby covenants and agrees
with the Association as follows:

1. THE CORPORATION shall be a trustee within the meantime of
The Trustee Act for the purpose of holding title of the above
lands for the Association and others as hereinafter provided.

2. THE ASSOCIATION shall be entitled to the exclusive control
of the said lands for the purposes of the Association as a summer camp for boy scouts, girl guides, or other groups of boys,
girls and young people of Huntsville and vicinity, and the
arrangements to be made in this respect shall be under the
sole jurisdiction of the Association.

3. DURING such time as the Association is in possession of
the said lands under clause two, it shall be responsible for

126

all taxes, rates, local improvements, public utilities and
other carrying charges as well as fire insurance coverage on
any buildings that may be on the said lands.

4. ANY buildings that may be erected on the said lands shall
vest in the Corporation and shall thenceforth be dealt with
according to the terms hereof.

5. DURING such period as the Association is in possession
of the said lands as aforesaid it shall indemnify and save
harmless the Corporation of and from any claims, suit
demands or any other liability whatsoever arising out of or
in connection with the said lands or their use.

6. IF at any time it should appear that the Association has
ceased to operate the said lands actively as a summer camp,
the council of the Corporation of the Town of Huntsville may,
at a regular meeting, consider the question, and, if in its
sole discretion it is deemed justified, a resolution may be
passed by the council in the usual way to that effect, following which the right of the Association to use, control and
operate the camp shall forthwith cease and be determined, except as hereinafter provided.

7. AFTER a resolution pursuant to the immediately preceding
clause has been passed, the said Corporation shall continue to
hold the said lands in trust as a summer camp for Boy Scouts,
Girl Guides, and other groups of boys, girls and young people of
Huntsville and vicinity under the management of a board consisting
of nine members constituted as follows:
All Saints Anglican Church shall nominate two representatives;
St. Andrews Presbyterian Church shall nominate two members;
Trinity United Church shall nominate two members; and the six
so named shall nominate three further persons interested in
furthering the objects of this agreement.

8. THE MANAGEMENT and control of the said property shall
continue as aforesaid unless it is deemed expedient by the

- 3 -

municipal council of the Town of Huntsville that it shall
revert to the control of the Association, which shall be effected by a resolution of the council passed at a regular meeting
of the council in the usual way.

9.   IN THE EVENT that it is deemed expedient to sell the
property or any part thereof, such sale may be effected by
the Corporation pursuant to a by-law which shall be passed
for such purpose, provided that such by-law shall only be
passed at the request or with the consent of the Association
or the above mentioned board, as the case may be, whichever
at the time has the control of the property.

10. PROCEEDS of any such sale shall be used only for the
purpose of improvements on the remaining property including
buildings, if any, or for the purchase of another site to be
used for the same purposes.

IN WITNESS WHEREOF the Corporation of the Town of Huntsville
has hereunto affixed its Corporate Seal attested by the hands
of the Mayor and Clerk-Treasurer respectively.

THE CORPORATION OF THE TOWN OF HUNTSVILLE

CORPORATE SEAL

TOWN OF HUNTSVILLE

"R. H. Leigh"
.... Mayor

"V. A. Adamson"
.... Clerk-Treasurer

8.18 Mary Lake

8.18.1   Vision Statement

It is the ongoing responsibility of the current stakeholders in the Mary Lake Basin to ensure that planning and development occur in a manner that will enable future generations to experience the special character and serene natural beauty of the lake including:

The unbroken forest panorama covering the islands and rising to the steep and highly visible ridgeline surrounding the lake.

Clean water and unspoiled natural environment throughout the lake basin that sustains the broad diversity of flora and fauna of the water and land.

Continued social and visual contribution of the notable large and traditional properties (camps, lodges, islands, marina and natural elements) which feature prominently in the landscape.

Harmonious shoreline and back lot building development that blends into the natural viewscape.

The special quality of community living, typified by the historical village of Port Sydney, that respects natural, social and built heritage.

Well-managed community access to recreational activities compatible with the established character of the lake.

Active stewardship that educates residents and visitors and supports implementation of policies to achieve the vision.

8.18.1.1   The "Mary Lake Basin" is defined as Mary Lake and the first 1000 meters, adjacent to the lake.

8.18.2   The 5 Priorities of the Mary Lake Plan

To achieve the Mary Lake vision, the stakeholders have established 5 priorities. Each priority outlines attributes which have been identified and deemed essential to sustaining and enhancing the character of the Mary Lake Basin.

The 5 priorities are:

Ridgeline Scenic Panorama

Shoreline Development

Water Quality and Natural Environment

Prominent Traditional Properties
Community Living

The background and goals for each priority are outlined below.
8.18.2.1   Ridgeline Scenic Panorama
The Mary Lake Basin presents a naturally beautiful viewscape that rises from the waterfront to the ridgeline of the surrounding cliffs and hills. Because the lake is a basic oval shape with only a few shallow bays, there is a sweeping visual connection from all points. The topography of the panoramic view combines gently rising forest coverage and extensive steep rock terrain. The ridgeline is unbroken and there is very little obtrusive or intrusive development in the panorama.
The goal is to preserve the unique natural character and beauty of the scenic panorama from the water to the waterside top of the ridgeline around the entire, visible Mary Lake Basin.
8.18.2.2Shoreline Development
        The Mary Lake Basin contains a number of prominent rock faces which play an important role in defining the natural character of the lake setting. A notable characteristic is that the tree line is located above or behind barren rock face.
The goal is to preserve the natural rock face in prominent locations.

The shoreline development provisions of the OP Section 3 (Environment) and Section 8 (Waterfront) are very consistent with the vision for the Mary Lake Basin.
The goal is to encourage public appreciation and understanding of these provisions and to support rigorous enforcement.
8.18.2.3Water Quality and Natural Environment
Mary Lake has characteristics that present challenges in establishing and maintaining excellent water quality and a pristine natural environment. These include:
Mary Lake's position on the Muskoka River is downstream of considerable current and potential development within the boundaries of the Town of Huntsville.

The overall drainage through the Mary Lake Basin is extensive and the potential adverse impact on lake water quality is difficult to monitor and control.

Mary Lake has very limited adjacent wetland and lacks the associated environmental benefits which wetlands provide.

Some existing waterfront developments, dating back many years, have compromised the natural environment.

The goal is to improve and restore the water quality and natural environment to realize the potential for enjoyment and preservation of natural diversity throughout the Mary Lake Basin

D8.18.3.4 Prominent and Traditional Properties

Part of the character of the Mary Lake Basin is defined by a number of prominent waterfront properties that are prominent based on their unique location and site characteristics and/or their historic use. For many decades the sites identified below have provided a "Muskoka lake experience" centred on youth education, camping and family activities.

Prominent Locations:	Traditional Use Properties:
Rocky Island	Sister of Saint John Convent
Crown Island	Clyffe House
Raymond's Bluff (SW shore)	Camp Mini Yo We
Buckhorn Bluff (NW shore)	Muskoka Baptist Conference
Gryffin Bluffs (NE shore)	Gryffin Lodge
	Mary Lake Marina
	Pitman's Bay

The goal is to encourage continuation of the longstanding use and form of these properties to maintain the traditional character of Mary Lake.

8.18.3.5 Community Living

Despite its annexation into the larger Town of Huntsville many decades ago, Port Sydney has managed to preserve and enhance its many small "village" attributes.

The distinct character and history of the "Port Sydney Settlement Area" has been specifically recognized and defined in Section 6 of the Huntsville Official Plan. The "village" has many defining attributes including historic buildings, deep setbacks of the lakefront properties, a large public beach, a central community hall and a single two lane roadway that provides a promenade from one end of the village to the other.

The goal is to ensure that any development maintains the existing village character and ambience as an important feature for all Mary Lake residents. This character is reflected in the built structures, commercial activities and the sense of safe, communal living characteristic of a small village.

8.18.3   Ridgeline Area

8.18.3.1   The term "Ridgeline Area" within the Mary Lake Basin for the purposes of this Official Plan is delineated in Appendix 11 - "Mary Lake Ridgeline Area" map.

8.18.3.2   Ridgeline Area Policies

8.18.3.2.1   Within the Ridgeline Area, all development is subject to Section 8 - Waterfront Policies.

8.18.3.2.2   All development within the Ridgeline Area is subject to Site Plan Control.

All applications for Site Plan Approval shall address, amongst other matters, the following:

Identification of the location of the subject property on the map of the Ridgeline Area

Specific reference to the impact that the proposed development will have on the "natural" view from the water to the ridgeline

Representation of the natural vegetation and existing or proposed tree cover
Completion of a plan checklist which will confirm compliance with Section 3 (Environment) and Section 8 (Waterfront)

8.18.3.2.4   On prominent barren rock faces adjacent to the water, no development, with the exception of limited docking/boathouse facilities, will be   permitted.

8.18.3.2.5   Solid Shoreline Walls and Structures
Creation of solid shoreline walls or "in water" structures that break the integrity of the waterfront "ribbon of life" is prohibited.

8.18.3.2.6   Shoreline Alteration
To protect and preserve the "ribbon of life" (8.3.3), the creation of new shoreline land by adding fill is prohibited.

8.18.3.2.7   Waterfront Landing Facilities
   To avoid further fragmentation and disruption of the waterfront community, development of new multiuser waterfront landing facilities shall require an Official Plan amendment.

8.18.4   Prominent Traditional Properties
The identified "Prominent Location" and "Traditional Use" properties shall:
a) Be encouraged to continue their current use and/or form and
b) Be encouraged to ensure that any proposal to alter their current use or form is consistent with the traditional lake character.

8.18.5   Heritage Designation
A suitable "heritage designation" for the area bordering Muskoka Road 10 running through the Port Sydney Settlement will be encouraged.

Acknowledgements

No book like this would exist without the help of a lot of people. I am particularly indebted to the following resource people who generously took the time to provide material about the past of our fine community.

Resource People

Part 1 Anne Troak – The Brown Family + Appendix Five

Part 1 Michael Ball- The Kay Family + Pictures and Appendix Three

Part 1 Barbara Fawcett – The Fawcett Family

Part 1 Charlotte Stevenson – The Fawcett Store + Pictures

Part 1 Mrs. Cliff Wright – The Fawcett Store

Part 1 Bill Clarke – The Clarke & Ladell Families + Pictures

Part 1 Phil and Joyce Rumney – The Butcher Store + Appendix Four

Part 2 Janet Fisher – World War One + Soldier Information + Pictures

Part 2 Bracebridge Examiner – Muskoka Regiment January 6 ,1966

Part 2 John Gall – Grunwald + Pictures

Part 2 The Huntsville Forester – Grunwald Articles from 1901 and 1902

Part 3 Jane Garden – The Garden Cottage + Appendix Six + Pictures

A Collection of Documents
Florence B. Murray
U of T Press 1963

I am particularly indebted for the help, inspiration and friendship that Bill Clarke provided. He volunteered many of the pictures as well as the dozens of details that linked the stories together.

I thank my wife, Eleanor, for putting up with me as I developed the book and for her many helpful suggestions as she edited the book.

Ryan Kidd – Port Sydney April 2011

INDEX